Twayne's United States Authors Series

Sylvia E. Bowman, *Editor*

INDIANA UNIVERSITY

Joaquin Miller

JOAQUIN MILLER

By O. W. FROST

Alaska Methodist University

PS
2398
F7

 119

Twayne Publishers, Inc.   ::   New York

MANUFACTURED IN THE UNITED STATES OF AMERICA BY
UNITED PRINTING SERVICES, INC.
NEW HAVEN, CONN.

Preface

THIS BRIEF STUDY of Joaquin Miller is, for the most part, organized chronologically with emphasis upon main themes of each successive period of his writing career. No attempt is made to introduce each work that he published during his long writing career, nor even to discuss each poem in his better-known books of poetry. Only those particular works most admired by his contemporaries are discussed—and with illustrative quotations since Miller's works are no longer available in many libraries.

The object of this study is to offer a close view of Joaquin Miller, a view supported almost entirely by primary source materials. Accordingly, it is hoped that this book will suggest new and (hopefully) refreshing approaches to the man and his work.

Chapter I provides a base for the entire study in that it concerns the early years from which Miller drew or claimed to draw episodes for poetry, fiction, and autobiography. This section compares the legends with his actual experience and presents considerable new information from manuscript sources and old newspaper files: Miller's writings while a student at West Point School, Oregon, in 1854 and at Columbia College, Oregon, in 1857-58; his period of outlawry in Northern California in 1859-60; his editorship of two anti-Lincoln newspapers in Eugene City, Oregon, in 1862-63; his expedition against Indian raiders of Canyon City, Oregon, in 1864; and his separation and divorce from Theresa Dyer (alias Minnie Myrtle) Miller in 1869. Although these matters are of interest and of value in themselves, they relate to basic questions that arise in a discussion of Miller's work.

Chapter II is about the author's apprenticeship as a poet from 1862 to 1869. Poems on Western subjects are analyzed; those published in the *Golden Era* in 1862-63 are for the first time discussed. The chapter closes with an examination of Miller's first two volumes of verse. Chapter III raises questions about his popularity in the early 1870's: How did he win critical attention in San Francisco and London? Why was his work so appealing? What is significant about his popularity?

Chapter IV concerns Miller's preoccupation with ideal beauty in womankind in his writings of the late 1870's, and at the same time suggests a possible new source of Henry James' *Daisy Miller*. Chapter V, a summary analysis of Miller's poetry, fiction, and drama, discusses in particular the influence of Lord Byron, Bret Harte, and Mark Twain. Chapter VI considers Miller's last great adventure in the vanguard of the rush to the Klondike in 1897-98, his irrepressible optimism in old age, and his literary reputation.

Research for this volume was undertaken during a five-year period and initially with the assistance of a Shell Oil Company educational grant administered by Willamette University, Salem, Oregon. In particular I wish to acknowledge the encouragement of Dean Robert D. Gregg and Dr. Paul G. Trueblood of Willamette University and the many attentions and courtesies offered by personnel at The Honnold Library, The Bancroft Library, the Oakland (California) Public Library, the California Historical Society Library, the University of Oregon Library, the Oregon State Library, the Oregon Historical Society Library, the University of Washington Library, The Harper Library, The Widener Library, and the New York Public Library. I owe particular thanks to Dr. David Duniway, Miss Elizabeth Carroll, Miss Esther Sweeney, and Miss Joaquina Miller.

O. W. FROST

Alaska Methodist University
Anchorage

Contents

Chronology

1837   September 8, birth of Cincinnatus Hiner Miller on a farm near Liberty, Indiana: parents, Hulings and Margaret DeWitt Miller.

1852   Left Indiana with family to emigrate to Oregon by way of the Oregon Trail, arriving in the Oregon Territory late in October.

1854   Left family farm near Eugene City, Oregon, for mines in California.

1856   Lived with Indians along McCloud River near Mount Shasta.

1857   Fought Pit River Indians, witnessing massacre of them. Entered Columbia College, Eugene City, near the end of the year.

1859   Arrested and jailed in Shasta City, California, for stealing a horse; escaped before sentence.

1861   Partner in a pony-express service from mines in Idaho to Florence, Oregon, on the Pacific Coast.

1862   Editor of the pro-slavery Eugene City *Democrat-Register* and then its successor, the *Eugene City Review*. September 12, married "Minnie Myrtle" or Theresa Dyer at Port Orford after a weekend romance.

1863   Moved to Canyon City, Oregon, to practice law.

1864   Led company of miners against Indians who were harassing Canyon City and stealing horses and cattle.

1866   Elected Judge of Grant County, Oregon, serving until 1869.

1868   *Specimens,* his first book of poems, published in Portland, Oregon. Followed the next year by *Joaquin et al.,* a larger volume of verse also published in Portland.

1869   Divorced by Theresa Dyer at Eugene City; two children placed in the custody of her mother.

1870   Left Oregon for San Francisco, New York City, Glasgow, and London to find a publisher for his poetry.

1871   Published *Pacific Poems* in London; favorable reviews led to the publication of *Songs of the Sierras* and fame. *Life Amongst the Modocs* was published in London two years later.

1879   Married Abigail Leland, hotel heiress, and lived in New York.

1883   Moved to Washington, D.C., where they separated; Abbie returned to New York City. Theresa Dyer died.

1887   Purchased seventy-five acres on a barren hillside above Oakland, California, where Miller resided until death.

1897   Visited Alaska and the Yukon to report conditions of travel and life in the Klondike for Hearst newspapers.

1910   Published *Poems* in six volumes.

1913   February 17, death.

Joaquin Miller

ing four years younger than he actually was. True, he was never in Walker's filibustering expedition as his poem, "With Walker in Nicaragua" in *Songs of the Sierras,* suggests. His sordid experience in the Shasta City, California, jail did not end in the manner described in *Life Amongst the Modocs.* As "squaw man," he was loyal to his spouse as long as it was possible for him to live among the decimated Indian tribes of Mount Shasta; and as husband of the "Poetess of the Coquille," otherwise known as "Minnie Myrtle," he was the victim of an outrage against which he manfully never defended himself.

As for his being born in a covered wagon "pointed west"—the opening statement of the autobiographical introduction to *Poems* —it is both just and beautiful; it is true in a larger sense even if it is not literally so. His tribute to his father, Hulings Miller, published in *Memorie and Rime,* describes very clearly a nomadic early life because of the futile attempts of his father to support his family as schoolteacher, farmer, merchant, and laborer. His father was too generous to be successful, too helpful to every man who approached him for help. The way westward was the only way during the first fourteen years of the poet's life. From Union County, Indiana, where Miller was born in 1837 and christened Cincinnatus Hiner Miller, the family in desperation moved short distances to the West until finally it became a part of the migration of 1852 to Oregon. The family then consisted of Hulings and Margaret DeWitt Miller and four young children.

But even in Oregon the family was never really settled. The stresses of those years adversely affected the mind of Miller's mother. The older boys left: Miller to California, Idaho, and Eastern Oregon; and the elder brother to the Civil War. This older, favorite brother and an only sister died—both in 1871. His lonely father lived out his last years in and out of debt with only at the end the blissful assurance that one of his family had risen above the anxiety of debts and a meager existence.

It is Joaquin Miller "pointed west"—to an unsettled West— that underlies the restlessness of nearly all his life. Nowhere is the state of his mind more candidly revealed than in his earliest journals when at nineteen years he wrote: "At times I wish me far away in some stranger land where I had no home, no friends, no society, etc., nothing that this cold calculating world might call lovely or enticeing but there alone in the midst of death surrounded by dangers and cast upon my own resources, dependent upon my own energies for the necessaries of life it seems I might then be happy, that my restless mind would necessarily be more content, yet I know by experience it would not."[1] His "horrid uneasiness of mind" was from middle life somewhat dispelled by the discipline of authorship, the regimen of a writing schedule. That his formative years in Oregon, California, and Idaho were years of disappointment, defeat, and irresolution is clearly evident; these years provided him with the materials for fiction and verse.

II

Those immigrants who crossed the plains as late as 1852 to take up land in the Willamette Valley of Oregon faced certain hardships their predecessors of the 1840's did not know so severely. The large companies of immigrants of 1852 found fewer buffalo to hunt and less grass for cattle to feed upon. Cholera spread quickly. The Indian, aware by this time that the white man was threatening his existence by destroying game, was increasingly hostile. "It is a sad story," Miller said to fellow pioneers at the Lewis and Clark Exposition of 1905. "There was but one graveyard that hot, dusty, dreadful year of 1852, and that graveyard reached from the Missouri to the Columbia."[2] The Miller family entered Oregon in September, 1852, and passed the early winter near Santiam City, about ten miles south of Salem. It was here that Joaquin—then called "Nat" by his parents and "Hiner" by his friends—first saw gold washed from the ground. His father had given him permission to go prospecting near Knox Butte on the Santiam River. A pan of sand produced three particles of gold.

Hulings Miller took his family, ox team, and other possessions to settle a claim on the McKenzie River fifty miles farther south in February, 1853. The "house-raising," in which many neighbors assisted, took only a few days. Three months later the fifth and last child of the family was born—George Melvin Miller; by then

Joaquin and his older brother John were able to assist their father on the family half-section of land.

Neighbors thought Margaret DeWitt Miller a very proud woman. Mindful of DeWitt standards, she was always very properly dressed. Moreover, she worked hard to clothe her family properly. She planted flax; and when it was grown, she pulled, hackled, and spun it. With flax and wool skeins, she walked many miles to a loom on which she could produce a bolt of cloth. From her cloth she made clothes for all the family, including bathing suits for the boys. These suits were quite unnecessarily fashionable in a day when boys did not ordinarily use suits. Certainly the boys did not appreciate them; the unseasoned wool kinked and curled as it became alive in the water. Even so, Joaquin was devoted to his mother. When she had her "spells"—when she acted queerly—neighborhood boys did not dare ridicule her in his presence.

Joaquin was a fighter, and he loved a fight. He and his friends killed rattlesnakes on Diamond Butte. Here also, from tall oak trees, they watched bulls of rival bands of Spanish cattle lock horns. Equally exciting were the campfire stories told by "Mountain Joe," or Joseph De Bloney, a scout with Frémont, a tamer of Mexican horses, and a seeker of gold in the region of Mt. Shasta. When Joe, with his pack train, stopped near the Miller homestead one night, he captivated even Hulings and Mr. Croner, the schoolmaster, by reading and translating Caesar's Gallic Wars.

Such achievements of learning were thought well worth the efforts of Mr. Croner at the little West Point School, where a log was cut out for a window, where split cedar planks served as writing desks, and where boys and girls were kept carefully segregated on the playground. Joaquin's first known poems were written down in a journal he had started in the fall of 1854. He had not then (as he admitted years later) "learned to spell." The following verses, entitled "At Shool," are dated October 8, 1854:

> The day is dark and cloudy too
> And the Mist is eddying round
> My toes they ache you bet they do
> As I hear the chill winds sound.

The boys they whisper and look about
And Will his mustache twirles
And Croner he has now gone out
And I set and look at the girls.

And they look and then I grin
And I look at Will and smile
But there is Croner a coming in
And now I must study awhile

But then the windows have no glass
And tis cold dark and cloudy too
But then the time is hurrying past
And I have much to learn and to do.

And here Im called up to recite
My Cutter Arithmetic
For I must study until the night
Or get floged with a stick.

I guess when Im as big as dad
Ile leave this plaguey school
Ile make the teacher wish he had
Not made me mind his rule.[3]

Under the same date, Joaquin recorded views about a school debate on women's suffrage: "I was pleased to see the ladies of Oregon defend the cause of Woman with such spirit on friday last. It showed that the ladies of our school at least had some spirit, but I think it is the ladies of our school only. And I was also amused with some of their remarks which were not so dull after all. Among the rest it was remarked by one who said that if women could have a part in making the laws of our country there would be no Horse Racing, gambling, swearing, and, especially, Betting. And thus she went on until finally she became so excited that she gave us a barter for a Bet out right. Well it is just like a Woman. Say they will do one thing, and if they were permitted to take the Pulpit they would say the contrary before they left it. But thank my stars, they are not. And so we have nothing to fear from that course."[4]

Such a self-conscious pose of superiority is quite different from the trite, romantic protestations he made in a letter he never sent from California to one of his West Point School girl friends two years later: "You were rich; I was poor and I felt humbled to see the difference in our stations in life. It was for that that I left home. It was for to make myself thy equal in wealth that I left my peaceful home and kind parents and came to this land."[5] But truly, Joaquin did not in 1854 feel that he was making so great a sacrifice. On October 20, 1854, three days before he ran away to the mines of Northern California, he wrote a second poem in his journal:

> Oh let me go from what I hate
> Oh I do hate this quiet life
> That poets call so sweet
> Away, away from the busy strife
> With flowers beneath my feet.
>
> I hate the field and pretty flower
> And I hate the meadows too
> And too I hate the leafy bowers
> Of which poets make so much to do.
>
> I hate to smell the new made hay
> Or see the mowers mow
> I hate to hear the Jackass bray
> Or the bawl of the harmless cow
>
> I hate to plow or hoe the corn
> Or dig the troublesome weeds
> I hate to hear the dinner horn
> Or sow the garden seeds.
>
> I hate the quiet old school house
> And every thing thats there
> Down from the little old woodmouse
> Up to the ladys fair.
>
> Then let me go out in the world
> On life's broad sea set sail
> Then let me go where waves are hurled
> And foreign countrys hail.[6]

Actually, Joaquin, at sixteen years, emancipated himself from pioneer life in Oregon with less deliberation than the poem suggests. He himself called the manner of his leaving "awkward and unlucky." The circumstances were simply these: he and his friend Will Willoughby (the Will of the first poem) were rolling boulders over the bluff at West Point simply to see them roll and jump. A second boulder felled a neighbor's cow, breaking its leg; and, rather than face the consequences, the two boys fled—fled south to the "diggings."

Before the end of the year Joaquin had separated from his friend Will and joined Mountain Joe at his trading post on Lower Soda Springs south of Mt. Shasta. During the next five years, the two were frequent companions. No person other than his own father was a greater influence upon the poet's life. Joe's stories, adventures, and ideals are reflected in both the *Songs of the Sierras* and *Life Amongst the Modocs,* the two works that made him famous. Joaquin wrote in *Memorie and Rime:* "I can frankly confess that I have drawn on him and his marvellous stories, making them my own, of course, for all those years." Joe befriended Indians as Joaquin's father had done. Moreover, Joe lived among Indians, fought with Indians, and sought to create for them an Indian republic in the region of Mt. Shasta, even when this cause had become hopeless. From this period of his life, Joaquin identified himself with the underdog, be it the Indian of the West, displaced, wronged, and massacred by rapacious miners; or the Confederate in the Civil War; or the poor of many nations. From this time, he became a fearless, reckless fighter, even in opposition to officers of the law.

The wound he received in his first battle—the Battle of Castle Crags—was nearly fatal. In June, 1855, he and Joe were mining not far from the post on the Lower Soda when marauding Indians, previously attacked by a company of soldiers from Fort Jones near Yreka, set fire to the post and escaped with supplies that Joe kept there. Joe and Joaquin followed their trail, marked by traces of flour from torn sacks, into the foothills toward the almost inaccessible mountain refuge of Castle Crags. Joe then alarmed Judge Rueben Gibson, who raised twenty-nine white men and thirty friendly Indians. Joe himself raised ten additional men. Under Gibson's leadership, the party circled Castle Crags, stopping at a lake to await the descent of the marauders. As the enemy approached, Joe put Joaquin behind a tree and told him to stay there. The battle lasted for hours—how long Joaquin never knew. He responded to Gibson's cry to attack, saw one James Lane killed by an arrow that pierced the eye, saw Gibson drop his own gun during a deluge of arrows. Then, as Joaquin later reported, "An arrow . . . struck the left side of my face, knocked out two teeth, and . . . forced its point through at the back of my neck. I could hear, and I knew the voices of Gibson and Joe. They cut off the point of the arrow, and pulled it out of my face by the feathered end. Then I could see." He was expected to die, but Joe carried him and held his head all night. He was one of five wounded; three had died.[7]

In this first engagement of an intermittent war against Indians on the West Coast, Joaquin was left penniless, his own belongings having been lost in the fire that destroyed Joe's trading post. But after mining a year at Squawtown near Shasta City, he had enough money to equip himself with a horse, a saddle, a rifle, and a revolver. Of the mining camps of Squawtown, he wrote in his journal on July 7, 1856: "I leave thee for Yreka with a pony and rigging worth $100 rifle worth $20 & $5.25 in pocket. Hurrah for little me. In good health in good spirits. Whats to hinder me from being happy, nothing will, nothing can. The world may go as it will. I will still be happy."

But it had been a hard year. He had bought claims and sluice boxes, hauled sluice boxes, worked in cold water up to his knees, sold his claims, played poker, found himself often the loser, and hired himself out to others. Nearly half the days he worked he had made nothing. His earnings of $50 in October, 1855, had shrunk to $40 in November and to $22 in December. On January 1, 1856, he wrote in the journal: "One year ago I was on Humbug Creek, Ciskiyou County, California and on that day I took a review of the past year '54 and I said to myself if this coming year goes no more usefully spent than the past it will be a sin and a great sin. But it is so. It has been uselessly spent. . . . I will leave off my follies and try and be some one." On December 21, he had gone to nearby Horsetown "to learn what the chance was to enlist in the Niquaragua expedition; found terms not very flattering." It is obvious from the journal that he did not go—that he did not join William Walker in Nicaragua.

Though Miller gambled, he did not work on Sundays; he often wrote to his father and elder brother, and he gave a dollar to men worse off than he—once to a "sick digger Indian" and once to an old man. On March 9, 1856, he wrote: "I have dug and tugged, starved and economized the winter through and I could not this day raise the miserable sum of twenty-five dollars. Yes, here I find myself in this damed hole of Squaw town in poor health as I have been all winter without watter, no money to leave the place on and no prospect of making any." The following verses, written on April 5, reflect this same sense of failure:

> O how I wish I a goin was at home
> In the valley of the old Willamette
> And never again Id wish to roam
> Ile seal the assertion with damn it.
>
> Ile not have to live on chile beans
> Shortbeef and rusty bacon
> Nor work in mud and mire and rain
> And be all the time a shaken
>
> But have enough to eat or drink
> And best of clothes to wear sir
> Ile leave the beef to rot and stink
> And Ile have no chile beans out there sir.
>
> But when am I to get back home
> Im sure I cannot tell sir
> I havent half the chance to get back there
> That I have to go to hell sir.

But hiring himself out to others began to pay off: in early May he went to the Whiskey Creek camps to pay off a debt to the man who had sold him a young roan mare.

His troubles were not yet over: he lost his mare, and spent a week on a rented mule before he found her. Twice on this hunt he was refused bread that he could not pay for: "I arose from the table and left the house. I first curst the whole set, then I pitied them, then I laughed at the affair, fixed up my old slouched and torn hat, tied up my patched old duck breeches that I had worn for the last six months & had patched almost every Sunday. Improved my old flannel shirt as well as I could." Leaving his mare to be pastured at a ranch, he returned at the end of June to be told that his mare had been taken to the States. But Joaquin and "some of the Squaw town boys" forced out the truth that the mare was being kept some eight miles away.

Joaquin's manner of leaving Squawtown supports the tradition of Owen Wister's Western hero, the Virginian. Disenchanted by his old partner Volney Abbey, Joaquin circulated the following lampoonery:

> Ye poets will open wide your eyes
> Excuse me for being gabby
> For I write of the renown of a man in town
> By the name of Volney Abbey.
>
> Wise Dr Gates thus speaks and prates
> Though you know he is somewhat gabby
> I been bereft of some flour I left
> I believe by Volney Abbey.

Volney Abbey "seemed greatly annoyed" and accused him "of being the author in such a way that [he] could not well deny. For," wrote Joaquin candidly and to the point, "I was the author."

Joaquin finished a leisurely bath in the reservoir and returned to camp to find that Volney had written a card "accusing the writer of said poetry of everything that was wrong." To the great surprise of all his friends, Joaquin wrote on the card, "I am the author, Hiner Miller." Soon "the pompous advance of Abbey was noticed. He carried a double-barreled shotgun and was accompanied by Gomes, J. and P. Mc." Then, wrote Joaquin, "I met him unarmed. I told him I was the author of the piece that amazed him so badly. After talking pretty rough with him some time while he made the air blue with curses I left him [and] set him down in my mind as a notorious coward."[8]

One day out of Squawtown, Joaquin met Joe De Bloney at Portuguese Flat and headed with him for Lower Soda Springs. Then he proceeded to Squaw Valley where he passed the winter with the Indians until the outbreak of the Pit River massacre early in 1857. Hay had been set fire by Indians in the Pit River Valley, and white men were shot down as they sought to escape to Yreka through the snow. Even though Joaquin was sixty miles away, he feared that he would be accused of having directed the massacre. With two Indian friends, he journeyed to Bald Mountain near Shasta, from which he reconnoitered the valley. "Indian campfires," he wrote, "began to gleam about the green and wooded girdle of the valley." He then spied upon one camp, but was met by two Indian women when attempting to steal away. These he and his friends made captives, but one escaped. Soon the whole camp was in pursuit; Joaquin and his comrades jumped into the McCloud River and hung on to a dry log that bore them unseen downstream to a point where they could swim to safety.

Mountain Joe persuaded Joaquin that he must go to Yreka to break the news of the massacre. There he was treated roughly, interrogated, and forced to join a fighting force that marched slowly a hundred miles to the Pit River Valley where they were joined by two companies from Red Bluff. Although the Indians had been given the promise of peace, starving bands of them were slaughtered in vengeance; and the Pit River Valley became a Valley of Death—as indeed the surviving Indians afterward called it. Then, as Joaquin was to write twenty-six years later, "As we neared the region of my cabin, far away toward Soda Springs, I bade farewell to the best members of the hated expedition and rode away. Soon a half-dozen shots told me that I had been ambushed by these same roughs. My right arm was broken, and my flesh torn in many places." Luckily, Joaquin, pressing his spurs into his mule, escaped to his Indian friends under the cover of night.[9] He remained with them, convalescing, until November when he made a visit to his Oregon home.

Joaquin, through all these years, had been conscious of a proud inheritance: "I will teach my noble soul to live as it was bred" he once wrote in his journal. Through the Pit River expedition, he had carried a copy of Caesar's Gallic Wars, reading through it with the help of a man who had been to college. His family perhaps easily persuaded him to enroll at new Columbia College which his elder brother was already attending. Having opened in 1855, the college had already survived a fire that had destroyed its first building on a hill south of Eugene City. A large stone building, Joaquin declared it "never had any plaster on its ugly walls and nearly froze us to death with its hard, cold dignity."[10] A fire on February 26, 1858, that gutted the building scattered many students who never returned.

Among these was Joaquin Miller, even though he was to proclaim in Europe that he was a graduate of Columbia College. His youngest brother even claimed to remember some of Joaquin's valedictory verses. Joaquin's college career lasted two or at most three months. During this period he used his journal for rough drafts of debates, for recording the vocabulary of Indians living on the Sacramento River, and for the practicing of calligraphy. Only on December 27, 1857, does he reflect upon his past: "I was anxious for war and yet when it came I was still restless and wished for battle and when this came I rushed like a maniac into its midst and then for the first time in life was content until struck down by the desperate foe. Then again . . . I wished me home. That madening impatience and restless disposition settled upon me with almost unresisting force. Recovered from this I determined to betake my self to the mountains to quit all civilized life, all society save that of the red man of the forest. Two years of the suniest part of life was passed in the snow covered peaks of the Sieras . . . far from the din of the old sledge."[11] Joaquin, however, did not return immediately to California. He taught school for a few months near Vancouver, Washington Territory, prospected on the Lewis River, and then closed his school when gold was discovered on the Fraser River.

By June, 1859, Joaquin had rejoined his Indian friends in Shasta County, a diminishing tribe that had often resorted to theft to maintain itself. When the ammunition was spent and when Joaquin headed for Shasta City to buy gunpowder, he was riding on a mule worth $80, stolen on June 10 from J. S. P. Bass.[12] Apprehended, he was arrested and committed, in default of $500 bail, to the Shasta City jail, a place so crowded and filthy that a Grand Jury the very next month ordered it cleansed, repaired, and enlarged.[13] However, on July 2, before trial, Joaquin and a cellmate escaped by sawing through the iron bars in the window while all the city was distracted by a circus performance. The *Shasta Courier* of July 9, 1859, commented editorially: "We understand they left rather a saucy letter to the Sheriff, which contained sundry quotations from the Scriptures in justification of the action. If they but leave the County and State, we may congratulate ourselves upon our easy riddance of the facetious jail-birds."

From whom did the saw come? Probably from his Indian friends, and possibly from Paquita, his Indian squaw, with whom he now took up residence with a small band of McCloud River Indians living in a gulch on the east side of Mount Shasta. In his *Life Amongst the Modocs*, Joaquin relates an unlikely story of a pursuit in which Paquita is fatally shot while swimming with him across a river. This story, often reprinted, had great appeal to sentimental readers. Needless to say, Paquita survived to share with Joaquin and their baby girl[14] the shelter of a small log house twelve by fourteen feet, with dirt roof and earthen floor and set amidst a half-dozen wickiups. Dressed as a Spanish vaquero with sombrero and red silken sash, Joaquin lived on a diet of trout and venison and herded horses for a pittance. Now his old cronies could dub him "Joaquin" after the colorful Mexican bandit, Joaquin Murietta.

In desperation he left his menage to look for a new situation in the vicinity of Yreka. After several days, he agreed to work for three dollars a day as a cook in a new mining camp ten miles west of town. Joaquin and the seven miners working the claim agreed to wait for their money until the mine began producing; by the end of two months, the owner was paying the miners but was ignoring the pleas of his cook. One day, when the owner and his men were at work on the claim, Joaquin hitched a span of horses used to haul drift timber and sold the team in the town of Deadwood to the highest bidder. Returning to the camp, he gave the money to his astonished boss after deducting his own wages. To threats of arrest, Joaquin said nothing. He simply rolled up his blankets, shouldered his rifle, and started down the creek with his two horses. Passing by the miners who sympathized with him and admired his daring, he started up a hillside trail; he had reached a point a hundred feet above the creek when a constable came riding up on a bronco and ordered him to stop. When Joaquin replied that he was not stopping, the constable cocked his revolver. Joaquin dropped his rifle into the hollow of his arm and faced the constable:

"Do you defy the law?"
"I defy *you*."

The constable fired, the shot passing through the young man's coat sleeve. Joaquin fired, the officer clasped his hand to his left side and fell to the ground. Assured that the wound was not serious, he left the constable in custody of the miners, mounted his saddled horse and, leading the other, proceeded leisurely toward Oregon.[15] Meanwhile, on January 7, 1860, Judge A. M. Rosborough of the Siskiyou County Court of Sessions issued a bench warrant, ordering "Hiner Miller be admitted to bail in the sum of two thousand dollars" for "assault with an intent to commit murder."[16] He was now indeed "Joaquin."

III

Back in Oregon, Joaquin worked with a party surveying a few townships on the south bank of the Columbia River. When the work was completed after several months, he returned to his father's home near Eugene, taught school, and studied law under George Williams, later Attorney General in the administration of President U.S. Grant. Though he was never formally admitted to the Oregon bar, Joaquin hoped to develop a practice in the new mining town of Oro Fino, Idaho, to which he went in the spring of 1861. Failing in this attempt, he and two brothers and several cousins moved over the mountains to the east, built cabins, made sluice-boxes, and mined with moderate success. When he had acquired a number of horses, he worked for Isaac Mossman, who by 1861 had started a pony-express service extending all the way from the Oro Fino mines to the Oregon coast. Joaquin acquired considerable fame as the best of horse-men, a picturesque solitary figure wearing the garb of a Spanish bandit, and a dependable expressman whose route extended from Oro Fino to Walla Walla and from Walla Walla to Florence, Oregon (Millersburg, as it was then known). Joaquin had become a partner with Mossman by the time Wells Fargo bought the business early in the spring of 1862.

He then returned to the Willamette Valley, bought his parents a home in Eugene City, and in April invested the rest of his profits in the Eugene City *Democratic Register.* This weekly paper, one of several hundred short-lived, four-page pioneer newspapers in the West, was founded by Anthony Noltner to support the cause of secessionists among Oregon Democrats. The first number was published on March 15, 1862 (subscription at $2.50 per annum), with Noltner as "Proprietor." Soon afterward, the proprietors were cited as "Noltner & Miller" with "C.H. Miller" as "Editor."

Noltner was the publisher of many newspapers, including a predecessor called the *Oregon Union.* The following notice, dated March 15, 1862, and entitled "PAY THE PRINTER!" was run repeatedly in the new *Register:* "All persons are hereby notified, that unless immediate payment is made for subscription to the *Oregon Union,* to the 3d of Feb., 1861, to the under-signed, I shall make out a *Black List,* and publish to the world every man's name who is mean enough to cheat the publishers of newspapers. . . . To me it amounts to upwards of two thousand dollars. This amount I need and must have."[17] Noltner apparently appreciated Joaquin's investment of several thousand dollars and his eloquent editorials far more than he appreciated his poetry. Years later he declared that Joaquin, if given free rein, would have filled nearly all columns with verse.

But the poet began modestly enough. An early editorial notes with regret a Union victory in a great battle: "The eager people inquire how many killed? We answer thousands; they are wild with delight, their minds have drank the most baneful poison to the moral man, and they only arouse from its influence to long and listen for something more terrible." Four weeks later, on the first page of the June 26 issue, appeared a sentimental poem with conventional imagery, but with enough restraint to suggest Joaquin's own awareness of his parents and of his elder brother John, who was to leave home to fight in the Civil War. He called it "After All."

> The apples are ripe in the orchard,
>   The work of the reaper is done,
> And golden woodlands redden
>   In the blood of the dying sun.
>
> At the cottage door the grandsire
>   Sits pale in his easy chair,
> While the gentle wind of twilight
>   Plays with his silver hair.
>
> A woman is kneeling beside him,
>   A fair young head is prest,
> In the first wild passion of sorrow,
>   Against his aged breast.
>
> And far from over the distance
>   The faltering echoes come.
> Of the flying blast of trumpet
>   And the rattling roll of drum.
>
> And the grandsire speaks in a whisper—
>   "The end no man can see;
> But we give him to his country,
>   And we give our prayers to Thee."
>
> The violets star the meadows,
>   The rose-buds fringe the door,
> And over the grassy orchard
>   The pink white blossoms pour.
>
> But the grandsire's chair is empty,
>   The cottage is dark and still;
> There's a nameless grave in the battle-field
>   And a new one under the hill.
>
> And a pallid, tearless woman
>   By the cold hearth sits alone,
> And the old clock in the corner
>   Ticks on with a steady drone.

Such expression of pacifism from a former Indian fighter and outlaw had its inspiration from his father's Quaker spirit: Joaquin saw the abolitionist North as the aggressor in the Civil War and the Confederacy as the underdog. Yet, curiously, other members of his immediate family were Republicans and supporters of Lincoln. His brother John served in the armies of U. S. Grant.

During the last month of the *Register,* Joaquin rose almost a single voice in Oregon against the scorn of his critics and against censorship of "treasonous" journals such as his. In the August 30, 1862, issue, he sounded the alarm: "The wild tide of affairs forbid silence." America, he said, was "now plunging into a vortex of oblivion . . . day by day becoming an enslaved nation." He declared that "Federal spies" were "placed at every man's elbow," that free men were being denied free speech under threat of prison. With all the passionate splendor of an orator speaking directly to a nationwide audience, Joaquin continued by appealing to the heavens and to history:

> Let us pause, and looking up, reverently up, to the great guardian angel guiding the destinies of nations, ask "Watchman, what of the night?" Americans have read of the ancient glory of Greece and Rome and wondered why such freemen did not firmly oppose the first encroachments of their liberties, and hurl the tyrants from their places of power. But the American sees now plainly how it came. Little by little powers were usurped. One by one the people allowed their rulers to steal away the sacred rights of freemen, and we now see these ancient empires peopled by a race of slaves. The ships have disappeared from their harbors, their orators have left the forum forever, their patriotic songs are still, their monuments are tottering to decay and the owls sit undisturbed in the now forsaken halls of freedom.

Lincoln, he concluded, would never resign the Presidency "unless hurled from it by the indignant people of the West."

Strange language for a pacifist! Reaction was immediate. A young printer, Henry Cummins, a friend of the Miller family and an admirer of Joaquin's sister Ella, noted in his diary under the date of September 3: "Worked in the treason grinding Register Office all day."[18] The next day, after only a week of setting type for the *Register,* Cummins abruptly terminated his employment and left town. Asahel Bush—a Democrat—and editor of the influential *Oregon Statesman* established in the capital city of Salem, cited a few sentences from the editorial and remarked. "The name of the miscreant and traitor who uttered the above quotation is C. H. Miller. As soon as his one-horse paper is busted up he will be found skedadling to the Southern Confederacy."

The young editor quickly retorted, "Traitor do you say? You cowardly, perjured, lantern-jawed, green-eyed Yankee—traitor to what? . . . Scream 'traitor' because a man dares to hope for the return of the peace and prosperity of our country." However, in the same issue of September 27, Joaquin, in a long editorial, is hardly an apostle of peace in threatening dire consequences if freedom of the press is denied in Oregon: "The Democracy in this State has done everything in its power to preserve peace, but forbearance *may* cease to be a virtue. It will not surrender its people without legal process, even though that determination drenches our valley in blood and blots the white race from the shores of the Pacific." But such freedom was denied by request of General George Wright, Commanding Officer of the Department of the Pacific. On October 2, he called upon San Francisco Postmaster S. H. Parker to exclude the *Register* and two other Oregon newspapers from the United States mails.[19] No shots were heard in Eugene City. After twenty-nine issues, the *Register* quietly ceased operation.

Meanwhile, Joaquin had married Theresa Dyer ("Minnie Myrtle") of Cape Blanco near Port Orford, Oregon, "the prettiest, freshest myrtle bough ever won by sword or pen."[20] They were married at her home at the mouth of the Elk River on Friday, September 12, 1862, by the judge of Curry County.[21] Although they had met for the first time only four days earlier, they had corresponded for several months. Joaquin was a pony-express rider when he first read a poem by Minnie printed in a small-town newspaper. He wrote her a letter which Minnie years later confessed she had "never been able to wholly decipher." She was not deterred; for, in a lecture given in 1872, she recollected the events preceding her marriage: "I wrote letters descriptive of the wild, romantic scenery . . . and then I told him of my own

desolate life, of my longing for a congenial spirit. I told him that
a delightful, dreamy trail wound over the mountains, and if he
would come I would ferry him over the river in my little boat."[22]

Joaquin was prepared to accept the invitation. On August 23,
the *Register* printed "Midnight Pencilings," a poem obviously
intended for Minnie:

> I am sitting alone in the moonlight,
>   In the moonlight soft and clear,
> And a thousand thoughts steal o'er me,
>   While penciling, sitting here;
> And the cricket is chirping, a chirping
>   And sings as I sit alone,
> In the tall willow grass around me,
>   In a low and plaintive tone.
>
> But fancy goes flitting and flying,
>   And I cannot keep it here,
> Though the crickets are singing so plaintive,
>   And the moon shines never so clear.
> Away in the hazy future—
>   Afar by the foaming sea
> I am painting a cot in my fancy—
>   A cottage, and "Minnie," and me.
>
> Now fancy grows dim in the distance—
>   So dim in the long since past,
> That I scarce can take the fair picture
>   Of the playmates I sported with last.
> But away in the western wildwood
>   In the woodland wild and wier,
> I relive in fancy my childhood
>   And sigh that I'm sitting here.
>
> Yet I know 'tis wrong to be sighing
>   And seeking a future too fair,
> Or to call up old hopes that are lying
>   A wreck in the sea of despair;
> I know that the present has pleasures
>   That I ought to enjoy and embrace,
> Lest I sigh for these days that are passing
>   When the future has taken their place.

Yet, as I sit in the moonlit meadow,
　　With no voice but nature's near,
Save the chirp and chime of the cricket
　　Falling plaintively on the ear,
I cannot control my fancy,
　　My thoughts are so wayward and wild,
That I ever will dream of the future,
　　Or wish I again were a child.

In the issue of September 13, the *Register* announced, "The editor is absent from his post." Joaquin, on horseback, had left Eugene City and, crossing over the coastal mountains, arrived at Minnie's home on September 9. For four days, Minnie recalled, they "lived in an atmosphere of poetry, and then were married."[23] Joaquin described her as "brunette, tall, graceful . . . of a very poetic temperament, and when we first met she was the better writer." The Dyers were not pleased by her choice.

The suspending of the *Democratic Register* was only a temporary setback. After a lapse of only one month, subscribers of the *Register* were furnished instead with the new *Eugene City Review,* a literary paper modeled somewhat after the San Francisco *Golden Era,* that contained "one or two original Stories, Poetry, and choice Essays, from various parts of this State and California," as promised by its salutatory editorial. At the same time local and foreign news was presented without political comment. The first number of the *Review* (November 1), far from offering a selection of "Choice Literature" from Oregon and California, printed instead two poems and two stories by "De Weiver," the new pseudonym of the *Review's* prolific editor, Joaquin Miller. In fact, with one exception, all the "Choice Literature" published in the Review from November 1 to December 27, 1862, was Joaquin's; and probably the single exception, "Trials of an Authoress," was Minnie Myrtle's.

One must even suspect the editor of perpetrating a hoax on the rival *State Republican,* published in Eugene and edited by one J. N. Gale. Under the name of "M. J. Briggs," he apparently submitted to this paper a somber poem entitled "The Departed Hero." An acrostic poem, the first letter of each line produces

"FANATICAL GUT, J. N. GALE." In "notes" to the poem in the December 6 issue of the *Review*, Joaquin concluded: "We shall always stand up for Mr. Gale. We know how much of other men's business he has to attend to, and know that with all that and the affairs of our government upon his mind, he cannot be expected to attend very well to his own. Yes, we like Gale; he is a good citizen, with big sandy whiskers, and is famous for always telling the truth when he can't help it."

Thus, the *Review* which, according to its prospectus, was "to avoid all comment of a political character," indicated its political allegiance by satirizing the editor of a Republican paper. With the issue of January 3, 1863, the *Review* hoisted its political colors; in an editorial entitled "Freedom of the Press," Joaquin showed all his old fervor: "We never ceased to deprecate the high-handed usurpations of power that forbid Democratic papers equal rights with other journals to mail facilities at all times and places, but we lived and labored in the hope that re-action would set in in the minds of a majority of the people that would warn the powers that be of the folly and the danger of too far trespassing the sacred rights of a free people." As for the goals of the Democratic party, they are noble indeed: "The motto of the Democratic banner we follow is, FREEDOM, freedom of speech, freedom of press, and freedom of the white man before the negro. It bows to the sanctity of the habeas corpus, and gives equal political rights to all men capable of appreciating the price of liberty. Woe to him who attempts to trail this flag in the dust and deface its mottoes; we will war with him to the wall, be he high or low, be he native or naturalized, be his name or nation what it may, he is the foe to freedom and the assassin and bitter enemy of Democracy."

On February 14, 1863, he announced his resignation from the editorship of the *Review*. He stated in his "Valedictory" that he had fought the Confiscation Law, the introduction of greenbacks, political arrests, suppression of the press, and the drafting of Oregon men to fight against the South. Reviewing his ten-months' career as an Oregon newspaper editor, he proudly asserted: "We entered the field when no other Democratic paper in the State was in circulation, and when the party was defeated and discouraged; we leave the arena with the party high in the ascendant, full of hope, and well supplied with able and fearless organs." Asahel Bush, in Salem, was also congratulatory: "Mr. Miller has made a very efficient editor. The advertisements were always well conducted, and the marriages and deaths ably recorded."

Political tensions had been much eased. Joaquin was correct in his assumption that the Lincoln administration would not persecute the *Review:* three weeks after Joaquin resumed open support of the Democratic party, the U.S. mails were re-opened to "disloyal" newspapers. His views had wide and respected support in Oregon; and with his withdrawal from the *Review* he "skedadled" not to the South but to San Francisco, the literary and cultural center of the West Coast. He and Minnie would go "for a time at least" to benefit from the milder climate. Joaquin had had a "serious illness" late in December, a recurrence perhaps of his illness of the previous July when the *Register* for three consecutive weeks reported that "The editor is absent from his post." It was no secret, however, that both Joaquin and Minnie had literary ambitions that had been much encouraged by recent acceptance of poems and sketches for publication in the *Golden Era,* the principal literary paper in the West to which Bret Harte, Mark Twain, and Prentice Mulford were all contributing in 1863.

Before Joaquin and Minnie left for Port Orford to sail to San Francisco on the *Big Susan,* a farewell party was given at Hulings Miller's home. Among those in attendance was none other than J. N. Gale of the *State Republican.* Writing to Henry Cummins in a letter dated March 16, 1863, Gale reported that he had enjoyed himself "hugely," and added: "Hiner's wife is a nice little woman and she is working him over to quite an improvement. They are going to the Bay City to *'drive the quill'* for a living, won't they make it heavy? I wish them well but doubt their success among old hands at scribbling."[24]

Residing in San Francisco from April through August, 1863, both Joaquin and Minnie contributed poems and stories to the *Golden Era.* For these they were not paid. Apparently Joaquin did not even inquire about payment until after his "De Laine:

A Tale of the Battle of Gettysburg" was printed in August. The editor told him very gently that no one outside the *Era* staff was paid, except Mark Twain and Mrs. Hitchcock—and they got as little as $5 or $10 for each contribution. Joaquin was no doubt dumbfounded: since such famous local writers as Adah Menken, Prentice Mulford, Bret Harte, Charles Warren Stoddard, Albert Bierstadt, Fitz Hugh Ludlow, and Amos Kendall—most of whom had not even taken notice of him—were not being paid by the *Era,* he could not expect to live by writing for it.[25] He and Minnie moved from their rented garret at 421 Fulton Street and returned at once to Oregon. Minnie remained with her parents at Port Orford to give birth to their first child, a daughter Eveline Maud; Joaquin traveled on to Canyon City, a flourishing Eastern Oregon mining community. Once arrived, he discovered that he was not a stranger: friends and enemies from the old California camps recognized him immediately. But Joaquin avoided trouble. He took his law books out of his saddle bags, tacked up a shingle, and began the practice of law. Since he had few clients, he bought a claim and worked it himself.

Hostile Indians raided the city and its camps, and repeated expeditions sent out to engage the Indians were invariably unsuccessful. Finally, in March, 1864, the Indians had succeeded in cutting the city off from outside communication, had frequently at night shot hundreds of arrows into the city from the canyon cliffs, and on March 15 had stolen both horses and cattle. In desperation the miners sought to organize a large posse to recover their property. Failing at first to agree on a leader, they turned to Joaquin, of whose fame as an Indian fighter and horseman they were constantly reminded by his buckskin dress, his superb horse, and his two pistols.

Joaquin immediately appointed two men as lieutenants and began to train and discipline his men as the posse moved out in pursuit of the Indians. The tracks left by the stolen herds were easy to follow, but the horses of the posse found almost no provender on the heavily grazed trail. Near Harney Lake, a small cavalry unit commanded by Lt. James A. Waymire of the U.S. Army joined forces with the posse. For nearly a week the Indians drew their pursuers after them through the Harney Valley south to the Steen Mountains near the Nevada border. Only one small Indian camp was surprised, and only a few Indians were taken captive.

At last one early morning in the foothills of the mountains above an alkali desert with steaming hot springs, soldiers and miners saw numerous horses spread over many miles on the misty hills. As soon as Joaquin's unsuspecting men had broken from the ranks to recover the horses, the Indians arose from the chaparral, mounted these same horses, and attacked. Two men were immediately shot down at Joaquin's side. One attempt after another was made to charge the Indians, but they increased in numbers and in audacity. Waymire, who had succeeded in keeping his eighteen soldiers close together, probably saved the entire expedition from being massacred. As night fell, the posse retreated with its wounded, leaving many men behind unburied. The Indians did not pursue the parched and starving company as it returned to a grateful city after an absence of twenty-four days.[26] During the next five years of Joaquin's residence there, the Indians did not again harass the inhabitants.

In June, 1864, Joaquin returned to the Willamette Valley to visit his parents and to escort his wife and infant daughter to their new home. They went over the McKenzie Pass, driving before them a small band of cattle and carrying with them cuttings of roses and seedlings of fruit trees. He later wrote: "My ambition has always been to build up a little home and make a moderate living by raising something in a garden, such as fruit, flowers, and so on, and also practising law in a quiet way."[27] In Canyon City, he built a small house on Elk Creek land and planted the first orchard in that county. His wife described their Canyon City home in considerable detail in a lecture she gave in 1872. Joaquin, she said,

> . . . purchased a house and lot on the hill above the town, and this place for four years we called our home. This home was a marvel to the camp. On the side towards the town he built with his own hands a wall of boards, nailed closely together. . . . He said he built this fence to keep the chickens out. [Sunflowers] he cultivated with the tenderest care. The soil being fine, they grew to a wonderful height, and bloomed radiantly. . . . He had

them planted in circles about the door, and in clusters by the walk, and all around the well, and in long straight rows by the fence, and under the eaves, and throughout the enclosure these sunflowers turned their yellow faces toward the sun. The front yard he had devoted to the culture of vegetables—first a row of corn, then a row of potatoes; here a little patch of peas, and there a bed of turnips. Along the walk he had sown wheat and oats, and a few voluptuous poppies nodded with the golden grain. In the back yard he had some choice roses, which he had brought from his mother's garden, of different varieties. At intervals throughout his garden were planted fruit trees—apple, pear, plum, or cherry. A pretty little stream gurgled through the yard, and fell in gentle echoes down the sloping hill below.

Joaquin's small office at home was accessible from an outside stairway. It was furnished with a long table covered by a black oilcloth. On the table was placed a large family Bible. Bookshelves contained British poets in one row, American poets in another, Victor Hugo's work, Scott's novels, Latin authors, works of history and biography, writings of Rousseau, Voltaire, Bulwer, and an extensive law library. Visitors were not apt to stay long in this office. His wife related that he "arises when his visitor enters, shivers a little, says he is not well and feels chilly; opens the door of the stove and fills it with wood. In a few minutes the stove is red hot, and the visitor sits fanning himself with an almanac until he can stand it no longer, when he arises and goes out. The artist then closes the draught, opens the window, and resumes his work."[28]

For nine months, from December, 1864, to August, 1865, he practiced law in partnership with Colonel Thomas E. Gray. During this period, according to Joaquin's own ledger, a total of $2,280 was received or due. In a "Memorandem" to himself, dated August 12, 1865, he describes the association as agreeable, but concludes, "I will now run the office alone. I know I will prefer to be alone and then can have my own way and use my own judgment about things and the management of business." By the end of the year, Gray was a political rival for the judgeship of Grant County. In a draft of a political speech, Joaquin states, "Mr. Gray and I are not personal friends. . . . I sometimes smile at some of his excentricities and dislike some of his reckless expressions, yet I know his worth as a man and his abilities to sit as judge."

Joaquin was determined to win the Democratic nomination for the judgeship. If he failed, he resolved to move to some other county to run for the same office. Drafts of his first political speeches reveal an amazing bluntness: "I ask the nomination, first because I am competent to fill the place. Second because I desire it." In his speeches he appeals to voters, not as an Indian fighter, but as a Democrat who had opposed abolitionism in Oregon: "I stood out in the storm alone. . . . I stood alone when no other paper in the State stood up for our cause." He even declares that leaders of the Democrat party in Oregon made such promises to him that he could appear before the state convention and "demand" his "rights."[29] Joaquin won the nomination and was elected judge in June, 1866. Script records of Grant County show that he received $100 per month from that date until July, 1869.[30]

He was known to his fellow citizens as a writer who insisted on reading his poetry aloud, much to their annoyance. They thought he was "cracked." At the same time, according to one acquaintance, "He had plenty of red blood in his veins and plenty of deviltry in his make-up and a hair trigger temper." A story related by Thomas Brent, later a judge at Walla Walla, illustrates this last trait:

One day one of the other county officials, a confirmed practical joker, came into Judge Miller's office. He passed the word around and about a dozen of us dropped in to see the fun. "See here, Judge," he said to Miller. "You have had quite a little experience fighting the Indians. Here is a military problem I want you to settle. Suppose you and a force of soldiers were in a fort like this." He drew a square fort with a gate at each side. "Suppose General Grant with a superior force held this gate, General Sheridan held this one and General Sherman this one. How would you escape?" Miller stretched out his hand and pointed to the unprotected gate and said, "What is to prevent me from going out through that gate?" "Why, I am watching that gate myself," said the practical joker as he hit Miller's knuckles a hard rap with a ruler he had in his hand. We set up a shout of laughter. Miller was furious. He jumped to his feet and picking up his heavy glass ink well he threw it at the joker's head. The ink well missed his head but hit the wall with a crash, spattering ink over all of us who were on that side of the room.[31]

But Joaquin had his fun, too. During the quiet summer of 1865, when the gold mines were becoming unproductive, he wrote "Canyon City Pickles," a series of letters for The Dalles *Daily Mountaineer*. Even though he used the pseudonym "John Smith, Gentleman," he was widely known as the offending author. How he offended is clear in the opening paragraph of his fifth letter, published on August 25, 1865:

Canyon City is crowded just now, and very lively. Taking my usual stroll, about 11 o'clock this morning, before breakfast, I saw three live merchants, all busy, of course. Bruner was lying on the counter, tickling his cat under the tail with a straw. McNamara was sitting at the breakfast table, picking his nose with a fork! Felshheimer had finished his breakfast, and sat at the table quietly paring his toe nails with the butter knife! A merchant sold a pair of shoe strings last week, and went to his drawer for the change, but the thing had rusted in its place from idleness, and he had to use a crowbar to open it. He remarked *en passant* to his customer that we didn't have dull times here much, but over at Owyhee they had it bad.

Nearly everyone in Canyon City read his "Pickles" on stage day, the *Mountaineer* paid him $30 per letter, and one outraged citizen called him "the d--ndest liar in the State."[32]

IV

To Minnie Miller, the "Pickles" letters were a disgrace. She believed every respectable woman in Canyon City was indignant about their vulgarity. She had already become disenchanted with her marriage; her husband had been too familiar with George Williams' daughter in Eugene City; now he seemed to neglect his family in his constant versifying and practice of law. He was irritable, abusive, and cruel. To Joaquin, Minnie was a spoiled child who, almost from the first months of their marriage, predicted "wreck and storm and separation." She lacked his ambition. She had not had "such a strange, wild life behind her to haunt her."[33]

Two children had been born—Eveline Maud in 1864 and George Brick in 1866. In October, 1866, Joaquin had gone "home" to Eugene City for three weeks. Shortly after Christmas (on December 27, 1867), Minnie wrote her mother, brothers, and sisters that she would be coming with the children for a visit: "Hiner has business taking him to Portland and he will go with the children and me as far as Eugene, and we will stop there a little while and then come on." The weather had been cold. Her husband's health had been bad, "the result of too much confinement and study." But they had enjoyed Christmas: "Papa" had given them all dresses, one for "Brick," two for Maud, and a new calico dress for her. "Maud talks all of the time about her visit to see her Grandmas—'one,' she says, 'lives in town and rides in a carriage and the other one lives by the big ocean and rides on the ships.' "[34] The letter continues pleasantly without a hint of "wreck and storm."

How the marriage came to an end is suggested by Minnie in letters and lectures in the early 1870's, but how Joaquin himself described the break-up years later in *Memorie and Rime* (1884) is very different from the facts. According to Minnie, Joaquin, whom she still loved, had disowned their children and "ordered" her back to Cape Blanco. After obtaining a divorce, she and the children had gone to Portland (admittedly against court orders) because she could not endure the isolation of her mother's home, nor did she wish to leave her children there because there were no schools. In Portland, she lived over a Chinese laundry and attempted unsuccessfully to support herself as a seamstress. Then, winning for a time the sympathy of the suffragette publication in Oregon, *The New Northwest,* she lectured on her life with her husband in both Oregon and California—much to Joaquin's personal embarrassment and much to the detriment of his reputation. Joaquin said little to the press by way of reply: it was, he suggested, a woman's privilege to relate the story of her marriage. He gallantly testified to her beauty and talent. He was quoted as saying, "I have disputed nothing that she has said. I will dispute nothing and will allow nobody to dispute any of her statements. Please say that. The relations between man and wife are so sacred, so holy, that I would be committing a crime if I were to say anything against her."[35]

However, upon Minnie's death in 1883, he wrote sadly and compassionately about her: Minnie had sought him out, traveling from Oregon to New York; she also wished to see her daughter Maud, whom Joaquin had placed in a religious school in Canada. In New York, Minnie had suddenly sickened and died, and Joaquin had buried her—by this time they both had remarried. In the tribute he wrote for the newspapers, and revised one year later for publication in *Memorie and Rime,* he seemed to protect her reputation all he could. He insisted—too much—that "she was good all the time; good and honest and true in all things and in all ways . . . no man or woman can put a finger on any stain in this woman's whole record of life, so far as truth and purity go." According to him, their separation had at first been voluntary:

Impatient of the dull monotony of the exhausted mining camp, and longing for the sea and the old home that almost overhung the sounding water, she took her two children and returned to her mother, while I sold the little home we had built and kept together, the new orchard and lanes of roses we had planted together, and remained there in the camp, promising to follow her, yet full of ambition to be elected to a place on the Supreme Bench of the State, and I worked on to that end ceaselessly. . . .

But the poor, impatient lady, impulsive always, and angry that I should have kept so long away, had forwarded papers from her home . . . to a lawyer here, praying for a divorce. This so put me to shame that I abandoned my plans and resolved to hide my head in Europe. In my rage and disappointment I arranged with her lawyer to give her a pretence of that which she professed to desire. Yet I knew quite well that this was only a romantic and foolish freak that meant nothing; that she did this only . . . to get me to come to her, and that she did not dream she could be divorced unless I came to her when the action was brought. Nor could she, in fact. But a court was in session, and her lawyer, who looked to me only for his fee, entered the case, and then wrote to her and published it to the world that she was divorced, while I was sailing away to other lands.[36]

The records of the divorce proceedings[37] reveal that Joaquin nobly lied about Minnie. He did indeed take upon himself in nearly silent restraint a shame for which the American public and particularly his fellow Oregonians would never have so bitterly reviled him had he broadcast the truth.

On April 4, 1870, Minnie filed a suit for divorce in Coos County, later changed to Lane County. Her statement declares that there were born to them not two children but three children, the third being named "Henry Mark Miller," born in August, 1869. She declares, further, that her husband "wholly neglects to provide for the support and maintenance of said children," and that therefore she demands that she be granted a divorce and the custody of her children with a cash settlement for their upbringing.

On April 18, Joaquin gave this testimony before the court:

> In the spring of 1868 she visited her mother at Port Orford. I came as far as Eugene City with her. I had to return to Canyon City to hold a term of the county court & left her at the residence of my father in this county. She shortly after went on to her mother then living at said Port Orford. In the fall following she returned to our home at Canyon City. She traveled very slowly although the roads & her health were good. She stopped at nearly all the towns on the way. I think she was about a month making the journey. She could easily have made it in less than half that time. She wrote me she had plenty of means to make the journey but borrowed sixty dollars of the Hon. F. C. Sells on this journey at Portland, which she denied for about six months, but admitted it after he pressed the matter: on this same journey at the Dalles she borrowed money of Col. Kelly all of which I settled. After she returned she frequently spoke of a man named Hill in an ardent & admiring way & told me in connection with his name that she would not have returned to Canyon City only to get money and take a tour through the county.
>
> I came to Eugene City the March following & found she had stopped at the Renfrew Hotel about one week & that this man Hill was with her. Although my Father took her & the children in his buggy out to the farm, she immediately returned & stopped at the Hotel above referred to. I then returned to Canyon & gave her two hundred dollars & paid over one hundred dollars of her debts which took nearly all the available means I had & asked

her to go to her mother's which she cheerfully consented to & did do. This was about one year ago & I have not seen her since. I have not sent her much money since I think she makes a poor use of it. She sent nearly all the money I left her when I came to Eugene at the time last referred to, to Brick Pomeroy in Newyork City to invest in letters advertised in his paper. But I have sent her about fifty dollars worth of clothing &c. for herself and the children, mailed at this place with P. M. Patterson & about the same amount from Canyon City, and about fifty dollars worth of Books, Periodicals, Stationery, &c.

I do not think her mind or judgment sufficient to rear & control all the children. All her literary productions of any account in the last seven years I wrote for her. I think her mother a pure good woman & am willing to let her have the two oldest children until they are old enough to place in an academy & pay her a reasonable sum not exceeding two hundred dollars annually in gold to keep them, though my mother or Sister I think the more proper persons & would gladly keep them for nothing. I am not in health as plaintiff is & have not been able to tend to business in my profession for more than one year past.

As for plaintiffs prayer for money of me I will state that her father gave her one dollar, or one 50/100 dollars, I forget which, which was all she had when she married or has received or inherited. I have about the same means when we were married. I admit that I have stated to her Attorney Mr. Ellsworth that I have not treated her as a wife for one year past & did not intend to do so in the future. I do not claim to be the father of nor do I desire the custody of the youngest child.

In denying charges made in his wife's complaint, dated April 4, Coos County, Joaquin had asserted, "She is not a fit person mentally or morally to rear & have in custody the children named."

Also on April 18, one William Brown of Eugene City testified that the man Hill was "a gambler, black leg . . . and thief" who had been run out of the country, that said Hill had once boasted that "he had slept with her often (those are the words he used) & that she had given him money & wanted him to leave with her," that Hill showed him a letter from her in which she stated that she would be in Eugene in a few days. Brown asserted that he saw "Hill and her together frequently in the parlor [of the Renfrew Hotel] & up stairs in a bedroom."

Also, on April 18, Hulings Miller, Joaquin's father, testified that in the fall of 1868, he had found her at Renfrew's Hotel with "several strangers in the room, Circus men, who were fondling the children." He took Minnie and the children to his farm, but she would not stay and returned to Eugene City. Finally, two additional witnesses appeared, to testify that Joaquin had called his wife "a common prostitute" and had claimed that "he could prove it."

On April 19, the next day, the court decreed that the marriage was dissolved, that Minnie would have the care of Henry Mark Miller "until further order of the Court," that Minnie's mother, Mrs. Sarah Dyer, would have the custody of the two older children for four years, that Joaquin was to pay her $200 per year for the support of these two children, and that thereafter Joaquin would be permitted to place these two in school.

Minnie was not in Eugene City for the suit. Had she been, its outcome might have been more expensive for Joaquin. For, strangely enough, the court "found" that the defendant had "no money." As a matter of fact, Joaquin did have money—enough money to give his father about one thousand dollars to pay off a debt, as well as to pay passage to San Francisco, rail fare to New York, and passage thence to Scotland. He had sold his property in Canyon City (leaving, however, a county tax of $47.50 unpaid) and had collected his last income as judge of Grant County. Joaquin was relatively prosperous—and ambitious. Now that he had had a setback in his ambitions in law, he planned to use his money to seek fame again in literature.

CHAPTER 2

Choosing a Subject: The Early Poems

I

JOAQUIN MILLER, as an author, early found his subject; the Far West—his own observation and experience in it—was his chief subject for poems, stories, plays, and autobiography throughout his writing career. It was a well-chosen subject, one surprisingly neglected by settlers who contributed to scores of short-lived West Coast newspapers and magazines. Recollections of an Indiana home, death, friendship, and the heroes of the Revolutionary War were commonplace subjects for versifiers who continued to write in the Far West what they themselves had written about in the Middle West, or what they had always read about in schoolbooks and other publications.

It is well known that Emerson called upon American writers to write on distinctly American subjects. It is little known that Joaquin Miller called upon Oregon authors to write about Oregon, in the fledgling and soon defunct and now forgotten *Eugene City Review*. In the November 29, 1862, issue he declared:

Do you know that Oregon had ought to be the very heart of song and poetry in America? Ah, you look incredulous and think of the practical names of the Luckimute and Long Tom and Soap Creek, but never mind them, look at Mt. Hood. It is itself a Parnassus. Look at the Cascades with its dark brow of ever greens and beautiful hills. Look at the little knolls and buttes that lay stretched up and down the valley, covered with white flocks and fat herds, and listen to the foaming sea afar off that beats with eternal roar over rock bound shores, and tell me if this, our sunset home, is not a land of song and poetry.

The *Review's* readers, more interested in Civil War news and in Oregon politics, were doubtless inclined to pass over the appeal, but at least they were somewhat prepared for the publication of "Oregon," the first installment printed in the December 13 issue of the newspaper. Miller was in earnest; four installments, each about a full column, completed the poem.

Never reprinted, "Oregon" is Miller's first ambitious literary work. Artistically, it is not a successful poem, but it is little worse than some of his later poems that were once both widely read and highly praised. His chief problem here and elsewhere is verisimilitude. He rarely achieves it for the simple reason that popular romantic traditions lead him to falsify his own experience or even to gloss over it altogether. Subtitled "A Domestic Poem," "Oregon" is to be "Of actual life in Oregon/ Mixed up with butter, cheese, and so on." And the poem is indeed thoroughly "mixed up" not only with pathetic rimes (*door* and *shore* relentlessly bring on *hoar,* and in one instance *so forth* is most unhumorously coupled with *grow forth*) but also with butter and cheese so invariably imported from foreign sources that "actual life," long awaited, is never easily discerned. In short, the poem is not so much about mid-nineteenth-century Oregon as it is about eighteenth-century England; it presents not so much the observations of its author as it does the deistic philosophy of a complacent, earlier generation. It is significant that Miller uses the pseudonym "Agricola"; for although Miller (and butter and cheese) is from a farm, and he "boasts himself a farmer's son," *Agricola* does not suggest either a "domestic" or a contemporary farm.

The inexact quotation with which the poem begins auspiciously is from William Cullen Bryant's "Thanatopsis" (1817): "Far away where rolls the Oregon/And naught is heard save its own dashing." Although "Oregon" is here an early name for the Columbia River, it is the first use of the name in a renowned work; and its use suggests a grandeur appropriate to the Far

West. But any sense of grandeur is immediately lost by Miller's smug content that is comparable to the self-congratulation of that popular, early eighteenth-century English poet-clergyman, John Pomfret, author of "The Choice" (1700). Miller writes:

> November's winds in wild afright
> Come whistling round the door to-night,
> But let winds whistle wild and roar
> And let rains rattle at the door,
> And winter gather white and hoar.
> The little ones are snug abed,
> The stock well barned, are all well fed,
> The sheep well sheltered in their shed,
> And thank kind heaven we have no poor.
> My wife with social chit and chat
> Sits knitting in her easy chair;
> Upon the well-swept hearth, the cat
> Sits purring in her corner there,
> And I am cheerful, yes, content
> With all these comforts kindly given,
> And thankful, too, for mercies lent
> From out the bounteous store of heaven.
> Thus peace and plenty seems to smile,
> With me at least.

Given the circumstances of Miller's own desperate restlessness, his uncompromising wartime partisanship, and the poverty of his own family, one must wonder at a couplet appearing in the same passage: "I do not rhyme for that blind crowd/Who thinks the poet's home the cloud." No whimsy is surely intended, for he declares proudly with more impressive if "hasty rhymes":

> But he who on our hills and pines,
> Ne'er looks but feels a thrill of pride,
> Whose hopes and heart with joy entwines
> Our mountain streams or foaming tide—
> Who feels his home in this far west
> The brightest, bravest and the best,
> Above all else and other climes,
> I'll ask to read my hasty rhymes,
> And rhyme for him a thousand times.

Despite clichés, the sentiment seems genuine, and even though the poet threatens indeed to rime "a thousand times" (the entire poem consists of 729 lines), the reader can appreciate the truly Western overstatement, concluding,

> We might find
> 'Mongst all the famous eastern land,
> All that man's heart could e'er command,
> But here we have them all combined.

The ideas in the poem are commonplace. Miller praises primitive man whose "untutored mind . . . stirs the hearts of all mankind," much as Pope in 1734 had written in *An Essay on Man:* "Lo, the poor Indian! whose untutored mind/Sees God in clouds, or hears Him in the wind." Like innumerable Romantic poets before him, he laments the big city (Portland, Oregon) whose monuments will someday crumble: "For man and man's but rise to fall/And, nameless, fameless, pass away."

God in the poem is a nature god; Miller speaks of the "living God in all our mighty mounts," and

> We can look at thee in the heavens blue,
> And gather courage and strength anew.
> And when dark hours environ the heart,
> And the tempter comes with his cunning art,
> We will turn to thee in thy purity,
> And on thy proud and spotless brow
> Read our duty and destiny.

Even the scenes are familiar: the descriptions of his boyhood pioneer schoolmaster with his "birchen rule" recall both Shenstone's "Schoolmistress" and Goldsmith's "Deserted Village." His descriptions of the Willamette Falls, the Columbia River, and Mt. Hood could easily apply to many other physical landmarks simply by changing the name. His tearfulness in saying good-bye to the Columbia, his "dear-reader" direct address, his platitudes, and his references to classical Greek legend have little appeal nowadays. On the other hand, the use of dialect (*big uglies, tarhead,* and *land of Pike*), an occasionally striking image, and an enthusiastic spirit win appreciation for his "plough boy's pen."

Characteristically, Miller in this work, as in many later ones, praises his parents and their Oregon farm on Sunny Ridge above the McKenzie River; and the poem concludes much as Goldsmith's "Deserted Village" begins:

> Sunny Ridge! dear, cherished spot,
> Never thy name shall be forgot.
> Never that kind old man in his chair,
> Never that kindest of mothers there;
> Never that maid with the soft brown hair;
> Never the boys whose brave hearts are
> Formed a nation's fame to share,
> Shall be dim in my heart or dull to my ear,
> Till the gray mists of death have enshrouded my bier.

While "Oregon" was appearing in the *Eugene City Review,* Miller succeeded in getting a poem published in the chief literary periodical of the West, the San Francisco *Golden Era.* This poem, and others that followed in 1863, are the following: Sitcum Siwash, "The Lost Fairy of Lake Alkah" (Dec. 21); Sitcum Siwash, "Dawamish" (Feb. 8); Sitcum Siwash, "The Hunter's Home" (Mar. 8); Sierra, "On the Rappahannock" (May 31); Cincinnatus, "The Siege of Vicksburg" (July 5); Cincinnatus, "Cape Blanco" (July 19); Sierra, "Lake Tahoe" (July 26); Ned Miller, "De Laine, A Tale of the Battle of Gettysburg" (Aug. 23); Ned Miller, "The Patriot Dead" (Oct. 4). Indian legend gives way to the Civil War, and two curious pseudonyms are replaced by variations of his own name.

The editorial comment on "The Lost Fairy of Lake Alkah, A Song or Lament," would serve for each poem he published in the *Era:* "There are spots of pretty expression in this, and lines that flow smoothly. . . . In some other respects it is, verily, a *lame*-nt." Indeed, the editor, Joseph E. Lawrence, is too kind; the dead "fairy" has never had any life for her poet, as these poor lines indicate:

> But Alkah, not thy charms I sing!
> Fair, lovely lake—alone;
> My plaintive lays to one I bring,
> Whom erst, thou well hast known.

> Far fairer bloomed she than thy flowers,
>   'Mong which she grew and died:
> One dearer to me than thy bowers—
>   Forevermore denied.

Just where Lake Alkah is situated, just who the lost fairy is, just how the poet came to know her—these are all mysteries in a most inconsequential poem. In "Dawamish," an invocation, Sitcum Siwash never had greater need of the muse:

> Divine Remembrance! Mother of the muse!
> Oh, lend me thine aid! my soul infuse
> With the glowing flame of sweet, poetic fire!
> Awake my muse! Awake my silent lyre
> And lade with notes of ecstasy the breeze!
> Let float thy sweetest murmurs o'er the leas!
> Vouchsafe to me your aid, oh, Sacred Nine!
> Ne'er sweeter theme inspired a bard than mine:

Dawamish, one discovers, is not an Indian folk hero or an Indian god of creation: Dawamish is a "sweet Arcadian vale" that offers the poet "a humble and secure retreat"

> Where fierce Adversity's storm could harm me not, ·
> And soon I found my longed for peace and rest,
> In Resignation's bowers secure and blest.

The heavy personifications of these last few lines are less distracting than "Spring's flower bespangled" in a "radiant summer sky," but one sees promise for the poet in the couplet: "Around me came the wild deer of the wood,/And cropped—unmindful of the storm—their food."

Most of this sophomoric early poetry consists of rhymed couplets in irregular stanzas. In "On the Rappahannock," however, Miller experiments with the Spenserian stanza with fair success. In "The Siege of Vicksburg," the meter is utterly unsuited to such a ghastly scene as this:

> Some dogs were gnawing a carcass warm,
> That a wayward shot had sped;
> O pitiful God! 'twas a human form

> With a woman's hands and head:
> The ravenous brutes had eaten her breast,
> Ere the woman was fairly dead!

Unfortunately, the lady had turned down an earlier offer of marriage made by a Union soldier in the midst of the siege. In this unlikely exchange, the lady cried:

> "Tear the red and white and blue from your breast,
> Trail over the stripes and the stars;
> And fly you here to my bosom and rest
> Safe under the triple bars!"

And he—true blue!—replied:

> "Never! my heart and my hopes are here,
> A blight on your bars and pride!
> The triple bars may float on your bier,
> But never float over my bride:
> Come you, to this heart that does not fear,
> And this arm that is true and tried."

The maid—and the reader—is not impressed.

Regrettably, Miller continued such melodrama in "De Laine, A Tale of the Battle of Gettysburg." The tale is this time somewhat more complex (and the poem longer); but it has the same violence, the same sad verse. One suspects that in these battle poems Miller first acquired the habit of relating impossible tales in settings he never had known.

II

Between 1863 and 1868, when he published *Specimens,* his first book, Miller was too preoccupied with mining, Indian raids, a practice of law, and Grant County politics to attempt to promote a writing career in any aggressive way. During these Canyon City years, he continued to read the *Golden Era;* he copied final drafts of his poems in ledgers kept in his law office; and he continued occasionally to publish poetry in frontier newspapers which no longer exist in libraries.

He had little encouragement. Anthony Noltner, his co-partner in the two newspaper ventures in Eugene City, once declared: "If I had allowed him to do so . . . he would have filled my paper with his balderdash poetry."[1] Lawrence, the kindly, indulgent editor of the *Golden Era,* could not advance Miller's ambition to be a professional writer. Canyon City acquaintances were unreceptive; one, a miner, recalled, "He used to write verses and read them to us. We thought he was a little cracked."[2] By 1868 Minnie Myrtle, who had similar ambitions as a writer, was no longer his companion and mate.

His own story of how he came to write his first book of poetry appears in the Preface of *Specimens.* In the form of a letter to his mother, the Preface imitates biblical English: "On the rough edge of the frontier, walled from the world by the savage grandeur of the Blue Mountains, I pursued the rugged route of my profession. Then I fell ill, and down in the shadows the heart hungered after the beautiful and the soul went out after the sweet ideal, a dove on the waters, and brought these things. . . . Specimens they are, may be 'of the earth, earthy,' and have quartz and other things clinging to them; but I certainly believe they possess some of the pure metal."

Published by Carter Hines of Portland, Oregon, the book consists of fifty-four pages and two poems, "Loua Ellah: A Tale of the Rogue River War," and "Shadows," an overly long descriptive poem of mountain, stream, and ocean. The "pure metal" is assayed, if at all, in descriptions of Loua Ellah, the chieftain's daughter:

> Sweeter than the kiss of morning,
>   Taller than the tasseled corn,
> Rose she from her sweet reposing,
>   Like the rising star of morn.

A few stanzas nearly approach, in style as well as subject, Byronic splendor:

> More that's saintly, less than human
>   Never was in mortal woman.
> God had saved his best material
>   And had bottled all the good

> He had found in realms aerial,
>   In the intricate creation
> Of everything of name or nation,
>   Since an age before the flood,
> And had used in her creation
>   That material and that good.

Miller, however, never imitates the personal and social satire of Lord Byron; he remains an ingenuous, unintellectual "Byron of the Rockies."

Specimens had only brief notice in the Oregon press, and Miller gave away more copies than he sold. Few copies of *Specimens* now exist; Miller was careless about keeping books, even his own. One surviving copy bears the inscription "To my Mother, December 30.69, C. H. Miller."[3]

Though discouraged, he soon made a second trip from arid Eastern Oregon to Portland to subsidize again the publication of a book of verse. This second book, entitled *Joaquin et al.* and published by S. J. McCormick, has 124 pages and contains eleven poems of which the first—"Joaquin"—is by far the longest. George H. Himes, later to become a well-known Oregon historian, was printer for McCormick when Miller came into the shop with his manuscript attired, as always, in the colorful garb of a Mexican bandit, with "affected high top boots and . . . scarlet tie." Himes recalled that Miller often sat in the shop as the printing progressed, sometimes reciting from Gray's "Elegy" the lines, "Full many a flower is born to blush unseen/And waste its sweetness on the desert air." "Then," said Himes, "sinking his chin upon his breast, he would murmur, 'That's me! That's me!' "[4]

Canyon City citizens had read some of the verse now appearing in *Joaquin et al.* in its only newspaper, *The City Journal,* "published occasionally." It quickly identified Miller, the former Indian fighter, desperado, and pony express rider, with the Joaquin of the poem:

> What rider rushes on the sight
> Adown yon rocky long defile
> Swift as an eagle in his flight—
> Fierce as a winter's storm at night—

In terror born on Sierra's height,
Careening down some yawning gorge?
His face is flushed, his eye is wild. . . .
Such reckless rider! I do ween
No mortal man his like has seen.
All flowing loose and black as crape,
And long silk locks of blackest hair
All streaming wildly in the breeze,
You might believe him in a chair,
Or chatting at some country fair
With friend or senorita fair,
He rides so grandly at his ease. . . .

O never yet has prouder steed
Borne master nobler in his need.
There is a glory in his eye
That seems to dare, and to defy
Pursuit, or time, or space, or race.

Miller glorifies the bandit also as he dies,

Here lies a youth whose fair face is
Still holy from a mother's kiss.

Perhaps Miller was not persuaded to take Joaquin for his pen name until several months after the publication of the poem. Ina Coolbrith, a lifelong friend whom he had first met in San Francisco early in 1870, claimed that she was the first person to convince him that Cincinnatus Hiner was not the name with which "to climb Parnassus and be crowned by the gods." Besides, "Joaquin" would help attract attention. In a manuscript tribute to Miller in the Bancroft Library of the University of California, Berkeley, Miss Coolbrith further declares: "The first time he ever signed the name was in a letter to me, its giver. In my last interview with his dear old mother . . . , she said she had one grievance against me, and that was that I had given her boy a name he liked better than the one she gave him. She always thought Cincinnatus a pretty fine one, but since I gave him 'Joaquin' he had preferred and used that."

Miller boasted that he kept the name until it was "at least respected." Certainly, Joaquin Murietta, miner, monte dealer, and finally bandit chief in California from 1849 to 1853, was infamous for innumerable thefts and murders. He and several of his men were killed near Tulare Lake by mounted rangers authorized by the state legislature to put an end to his marauding throughout the state. Hated and abused by miners because of his Mexican origins, Murietta had pledged revenge against Anglo-American newcomers in the state. Shot to death and decapitated, his head was exhibited in various California communities.

In the poem there is no surprise attack of the rangers, no hint at the animosity of the Mexican bandit or of his attackers. Instead, Joaquin flees alone on his horse, falls fatally wounded, and—after thirty pages—dies in a church with a priest prepared to minister to him. Early in the poem, death appears to be imminent. Here he

> Is clutching in its iron clasp
> A clump of sage, as if to hold
> The earth from slipping from his grasp;
> While stealing from his brow a stain
> Of purple blood and gory brain
> Yields to the parched lips of the plain,
> Swift to resolve to dust again.

And much later, he is still not only alive but indulging in a quiet boast:

> I am no creedist. Faith to me
> Is but a name for mystery.

He is still speaking several pages later even as life departs, "I thrust—I fail—I fall—I die—," and the melodramatic poet cannot resist a trite summary:

> He bled—he battled—he ruled a day,
> And peaceful nature resumed her sway.

Through it all he keeps his dignity—and his head:

> Death has been in at the low church door,
> For his foot-prints lie on the stony floor.
> There are raven locks of flowing hair;
> The stole and the surplice too are there;
> And I have seen them all before.

Miller's readers as well had seen all this before—in countless Gothic tales and dime novels. The actual Joaquin Murietta is scarcely in the poem, even in the slightest detail.

Shorter poems in *Joaquin et al.* demonstrate how poorly Miller could write poetry—and he confesses his own disappointment. He has written "no thought . . . that lives." His lines are rough,

> Plucked from my mountains in the dusk of life, as one
> Without taste or time to select, or put in good array,
> Grasps at once rose, leaf, briar, on the brink, and hastes away.

This puerile verse produced by a writer now thirty-two years of age is crowned by an absurd address, "To the Bards of San Francisco Bay":

> I am as one unlearned, uncouth,
> From country come to join the youth
> Of some sweet town in quest of truth;
>   A skilless northern Nazarene—
> From whence no good can ever come.
> I stand apart as one that's dumb.
> I hope—I fear—I hasten home.
>   I plunge into my wilds again.
>
> I greet you on your brown bent hills
> Discoursing with the beaded rills,
> While over all the full moon spills
>   His flood in gorgeous plenilune.
> White skilful hands sweep o'er the strings,
> I heed as when a seraph sings,
> I lean to catch the whisperings,
>   I list into the night's sweet noon.

Though Bret Harte had obligingly reviewed *Joaquin et al.* in the *Overland Monthly* in January, 1870 (Miller had requested the "signal service and kindness"), only one bard of San Francisco was on hand to greet the self-styled "northern Nazarene" when he arrived by steamer in June, 1870; and this bard later reported that no sooner had he recognized the figure "clad in a

pair of beaded moccasins . . . and a broad-brimmed *sombrero*"
and exchanged greetings than Miller proposed, "Well, let us go
and talk with the poets!"[5]

Did Miller take himself seriously? In the main, he did. He was
too consistent in his dress and his wanderlust, and too persistent
in his poetic ambition to be a mere poseur. That he was taken
seriously by readers of *Songs of the Sierras* is a greater marvel—
and one that now deserves study.

CHAPTER 3

Autobiography of the
Far Western Hero

I

SAN FRANCISCO was not Parnassus. This conclusion Miller had reached after his fiasco there in 1863. He must go farther, to London, the literary capital of the world—but first he must make suitable preparations. These he made very deliberately now that wife and family were no longer a hindrance and now that his next goal in law, a seat on the bench of the State Supreme Court, was abruptly denied him by his own political party. *Joaquin et al.* was his self-christening, in which he no longer offered "specimens" to Portland and Canyon City but to the literati of San Francisco. This city was to prepare him for his entrance—to be the gate from which he would emerge toward a full recognition of his identity. This "northern Nazarene" dared to seek a new Jerusalem.

Charles Warren Stoddard was the bard to whom Miller revealed his "little plan." Stoddard was to get *Joaquin et al.* reviewed in the new *Overland Monthly*. Stoddard was to greet him as he stepped from the boat in San Francisco Bay, and he was to introduce him to the small colony of writers. Even though Miller had never before written to Stoddard, even though he was a virtual stranger to him, Stoddard did all that he was asked. He got Bret Harte to write a generous notice of Miller's volume: Harte heralded its writer as having a "true poetic instinct, with a natural felicity of diction and a dramatic vigor that are good in performance and yet better in promise."[1] Stoddard also introduced him to his benefactor Harte, newly famous himself and about to leave the *Overland* for the editorship of the *Atlantic Monthly* and continued adulation in the East. Since Stoddard was also about to leave San Francisco (he went to Tahiti and soon thereafter produced *South Sea Idyls*), Miller was left to the care and nurture of Ina Coolbrith, local poet and journalist.

"Divinely tall and most divinely fair" was Ina. To her, he was "a tall, fine-looking, blonde gentleman."[2] The sombrero and beaded moccasins were discreetly left in the hotel room when Miller went with Stoddard to meet the lady at her home. She learned at once that he was on his way to London, that he had with him "a large package of MS, and a larger one of ambition." She noted, also with gentle irony, his "modest intention" to receive there a proper acclaim.[3]

Miss Coolbrith, like Stoddard and Harte, served Miller well as a participant in a fantastic episode which, in the form of a play, might be called Ascent from the Wilderness, Act I, San Francisco. She took him about the city during the several days of his stay, arranged for him to write letters from Europe for the San Francisco *Bulletin* and the *Alta Californian*, hailed him as Joaquin, and on the day before his departure, took him to the hills of Suasalito to gather laurel. The wreath she made him that evening he attached not to his head but to his valise so that he might carry it all the way to England to present as an offering of praise to the great Lord Byron, whose tomb at Newstead was ignored and unadorned.[4]

The way was long and hard as Miller describes it in his diary, later published in *Memorie and Rime*. After a journey of seven days by train from San Francisco to New York City, he was reunited briefly with his favorite brother John, now failing in health and to die within a year as a result of rigors of Civil War service. The big city was a hateful place—a Portland, Oregon, magnified. On August 19, 1870, he took passage, second class, on the *Europa* for Glasgow. Thence, he made a long pilgrimage, first to the grave of Burns and then to that of Byron. Before these he paid tribute, reciting aloud such lines of his own as these most memorable ones:

> In men whom men condemn as ill
> I find so much of goodness still,
> In men whom men pronounce divine
> I find so much of sin and blot,
> I hesitate to draw a line
> Between the two, where God has not.[5]

At the church of Hucknall Torkard, Miller made a bargain with the sexton who was to see that the wreath was kept on Byron's tomb and for his pains was to receive a sovereign each year. But the vicar objected and an appeal was made to the Bishop of Norwich, who promptly "sent to the King of Greece for another laurel wreath and so had the two hung side by side above the bust of Byron, who, had he lived, would have been king of the land he died to liberate from the Turk. But the King of Greece did more than this, so did the Bishop of Norwich. So money poured in and the church was rebuilt."[6] Miller concluded that, because of the wreath, the dilapidated old church thus became a splendid new one.

From Newstead he ventured to scenes of the Franco-Prussian War then waging, got arrested repeatedly, and wrote the promised letters for the San Francisco newspapers. He then entered London for the winter. He discovered that seeking a publisher for his poems was an "impossible task." No money came from San Francisco for his letters, which had in fact been discarded because his handwriting was illegible. Money from his brother John was slow in coming. Then he got an audience with the great publisher, John Murray, who took the manuscript from him and without reading returned it with the comment, "Poetry won't do." Murray was Miller's last hope; he had called upon all the other publishers he knew about, and none would risk publication of his work.

London appeared to be the desert again where "Full many a flower is born to blush unseen." Miller pawned his watch to have one hundred copies of his poems printed, this time anonymously. And there was the same preface stating: "These lines were written on the rough edges of the frontier, amid the scenes described. . . . Where this was written, rhyming is considered a mild type of insanity. . . . I bring this rough quartz specimen torn from the outcropping of the ledge, to those who know gold from grosser metal. I am very much in earnest, and court a correct assay." Whittingham and Wilkins brought out the book, dedicated "To Maud," consisting of 107 pages, and entitled *Pacific Poems.*

Springtime and Eastertide! The *St. James Gazette* declared that the first poem of the volume, "Arazonian," was by Browning! With the help of friends, the poems were now revised and enlarged. New poems were added. A new title was settled upon— *Songs of the Sierras.* For the first time "Joaquin Miller" was printed on the title page. A big book of 301 pages, it came out under the imprint of Longman, Green, Reader, and Dyer on April 19, 1871. A number of London literary journals extolled the poet's "promise," much as Bret Harte had done earlier, and compared him with Swinburne, Browning, and Byron. Invitations to dine came week after week through the spring and summer; Miller met Browning and the Pre-Raphaelites and was thrilled. London society was enchanted by its "Poet of the Sierras"—sombrero, flowing hair, top boots, and bold manner. The ascent was accomplished: San Francisco, Newstead, London. How was it possible?

II

Songs of the Sierras and later writings of the 1870's that sustained Miller's popularity present the same image of the Far Western hero, and this hero in poem after poem is essentially the poet himself. The land and the peoples of remote America are incidental: the important point is the poet's saying or seeming to say, "This is me, and I was there."

In *Songs of the Sierras,* he is oblivious to William Walker throughout most of the poem, "With Walker in Nicaragua"; he sings rapturously of his youthful love for a Nicaraguan maiden, so much so that he concludes, "I know not which I mourn the most [*sic*] . . . My chief or my unwedded wife." Although in other major poems of the volume the Arazonian,[7] the Californian, and the Tall Alcalde all tell their own stories, they are alike; they unmistakably speak with one voice—that of the poet. The gigantic West calls for gigantic men capable of gigantic action and gigantic love. There is the Arazonian "down in a cañon . . . cleft asunder." There is the Californian "wheeling like a hurricane" on his horse and "defying wood, or stone, or flood." There is the Tall Alcalde "tower'd up" and "grandly tall" rising to speak, "Hand me! touch me, him who dare!" The West is

> the land where the sun goes down,
> And gold is gather'd by tide and by stream,
> And maidens are brown as the cocoa brown,
> And life is a love and love is a dream.[8]

Each hero has his noble brown Indian maid with her "black hair boundless as the night." For the hero, love is passion deep and pure: "Let the unclean think things unclean."

How did the poet come to know his heroes? Usually, he gives no explanation except he was "there." In the preface to *Pacific Poems,* he declares, "The city of Mexico was my Mecca." "Isles of the Amazons" in *Songs of Sun-lands* (1873) takes him to "Incan Isles." *The Ship in the Desert* (1875) takes him across the whole breadth of the great West. Lest there be any doubt about it, the poet claims in the preface to *Songs of the Mexican Seas* (1887), "The lines in this little book, as in all my others were written, or at least conceived, in the lands where the scenes are laid; so that whatever may be said of the imperfection of my work, I at least have the correct atmosphere and color."[9]

Whether Miller had actually been "there" or not—he had not been to Nicaragua nor perhaps even to Mexico and Arizona—he does not, in any event, particularize: atmosphere and color generally do not vary from locale to locale. He is not informative; the few details that he provides about any place or person are rarely precise. Walker, for instance, is described as "tall." He had to be tall to fit the heroic mould. Even if Miller had seen him in Nicaragua or elsewhere and had known that he was actually short, his shortness would not do: there must be truth beyond fact, truth despite fact. And the truth is that the Western

hero, beaten underdog though he be, rises tall in mind and soul
and—in the poet's vision of him—in body.

Heroes are associated with legend, and Miller provides
fantastic incident not from contemporary events or even from
history. Whatever the stories Joe de Bloney provided for *Songs
of the Sierras*, Miller fashioned them in his own repetitive chant-
ing rhythms, rhythms so dominant that the threads between
incidents become tenuous and the story itself becomes sub-
merged in the robust sway of rime. It is fantastic that the
Arazonian should tell his tale to a squire—unless, indeed, he is
Miller in England! The Arazonian has a fantastic dream:

> One time in the night as the black wind shifted,
> And a flash of lightning stretch'd over the stream,
> I seem'd to see her with brown hands lifted—
> Only seem'd to see, as one sees in a dream—
> With her eyes wide wild and her pale lips press'd
> And the blood from her brow and the flood to her breast:
> When the flood caught her hair as the flax in a wheel,
> And wheeling and whirling her round like a reel,
> Laugh'd loud her despair, then leapt long like a steed,
> Holding tight to her hair, folding fast to her heel,
> Laughing fierce, leaping far as if spurr'd to its speed.[10]

The dream is true! The Arazonian awakens to see her, still alive,
as "She lay with the wave on the warm white sand." Then suddenly (the reader is taken by surprise) he throws himself upon
the same white sand "Utterly famish'd, and ready to die," but
the good brown maiden valiantly carries him to safety before a
flood from the mountains sweeps through the canyon.

"Californian" is "Joaquin" revised and enlarged: its hero is
grander, leaving in death a vision not of some unidentified
Indian girl but "the last of the Montezuma's line."

In "The Tale of the Tall Alcalde," the Tall Alcalde, captured
in war and imprisoned, is set free by a beautiful maiden who
has built her own funeral pyre because she is "impure":

> She caught a dagger from her side
> And plunged it to its silver hilt
> Into her hot and bursting heart
> And fell into my arms and died.[11]

Dutifully, he places her upon the pyre.

As the setting of Miller's poems becomes more distant, legendary aspects become increasingly evident. In "Isles of the Amazons," the poet intrudes

> Where woman's hand with a woman's heart
> Has fashion'd an Eden from man apart,
> And she walks in her garden alone with God.[12]

In this place there are tigers as well as serpents and a Queen who is "strong in her will/Of war, and hatred to the touch of man." Nevertheless, love prevails:

> She led him forth, and she bade him sing:
> Then bade him cease; and the gold of his hair
> She touch'd with her hands; she embraced him there,
> Then lifted her voice and proclaim'd him King.[13]

In *The Ship in the Desert*, a book-long poem of 205 pages, the story is sheer fantasy: Morgan, "a grand old Neptune," with Ina, his bride, and his retinue pass by near Omaha in a low, black boat; they are pursued across the plains and over the Sierras by the mysterious Vasques; and they are slain finally on a California desert. Is Ina happy? "She turns, she looks along the plain,/Imploring love to come again."[14] She implores the love of Vasques—or of the poet? The poet loved her,

> Yea, loved her for her large dark eyes;
> Yea, loved her for her brow's soft brown;
> Her hand as light as heaven's bars;
> Yea, loved her for her mouth. Her mouth
> Was roses gathered from the south,
> The warm south side of Paradise,
> And breathed upon and handed down,
> By angels on a stair of stars.[15]

What of the Ship?

> There loom'd from out the desert vast
> A lonely ship, well-built and trim,
> And perfect all in hull and mast.[16]

The Ship may be the "island in a sea of sand" where Ina has a thousand birds but not one who "builds in her heart." Miller, never cryptic and rarely subtle, makes his point:

> The test of worth
> Is not the hold you have on earth.
> Lo! there be gentlest souls sea-blown
> · That know not any harbor known.
> Now it may be the reason is
> They touch on fairer shores than this.[17]

Like the mountain man about to tell a tall tale, Miller insists that what he writes is the truth about himself. "My poems are literally my autobiography," he once said.[18] As for his first important prose work, *Life Amongst the Modocs*, the subtitle *Unwritten History* promises a factually accurate account. But Miller presses the point. Like an Aphra Behn introducing *Oroonoko*, or Daniel Defoe *Robinson Crusoe*, he must say, "I shall endeavor to make this sketch of my life with the Indians . . . true in every particular."[19] When he adds, "In so far as I succeed in doing that I think the work will be novel and original," he speaks truly: the most disappointing parts of this long miscellany of narration, description, and reflection—of biography as well as autobiography—are fictional; these parts concern the exploits of two heroes, the man Prince and the author himself.

Prince is introduced early in the book, when Miller himself because of his youth does not yet fully qualify for a heroic role. Miller calls Prince "a man naturally noble and generous in all his instincts." In the mining camps, he is a man apart. The miners find him uncompanionable: he is "too fine-haired"; he never goes on any "glorious benders." He is a friend of the Indian, a friend of any underdog. He saves the lives of two Indian children during a sudden massacre initiated by miners, and he provides for them as their guardian. He saves the doctor, a foreigner accused of murder, from arrest and capture. Then Prince drops out of the story; he is said to be in Nicaragua.

A stereotype hero, Prince is obviously suggested by someone the poet could not have known very well. Whether or not he was actually one James Thompson (as Miller states at the conclusion of the book), one must suspect that Miller is reintroducing William Walker under the guise of Prince. Certainly, he would not dare to say so. He had been branded a liar because of "With Walker in Nicaragua," and he had lamely defended himself against the charge that he describes Walker as "tall" in that poem.[20] Later, in the presence of Ina Coolbrith and another person who had been in Walker's filibustering expedition, he was forced to confess the truth: he had not been with Walker in Nicaragua. Although Walker had practiced law in Marysville, he had left by the time Miller came to mining camps in Northern California. It is conceivable that the poet could have seen Walker in San Francisco or elsewhere in California early in 1855 before the adventurer left for Nicaragua for the first time, but it is highly unlikely that Walker could have spent as much time with Miller as Prince does in the first two-thirds of the book.

Miller reintroduces Prince in the autobiographical preface to the collected poems. He asserts that Prince, not Joseph de Bloney, was the planner of an Indian republic with Mount Shasta at its center. Walker, of course, was not interested in creating a state for Indians; he saw his destiny first in Mexico, where he vainly attempted to establish an independent state in Lower California in 1853-54; and later in Central America, where he eventually succeeded in having himself inaugurated in 1856 as president of Nicaragua and in serving nearly a year before losing a war against Costa Rica and having to surrender to the United States Navy to avert further bloodshed. His grandiose scheme was the creation of a military empire in Central America, one independent of the United States both politically and economically. By reintroducing African slavery and by building an inter-ocean canal, he hoped to prosper through trade with Europe. Walker's venture came precipitously to an end when he seized ships and other property of a company coming under the control of the powerful Cornelius Vanderbilt. Though Walker failed in his ambitions (in 1860 he was shot to death by Honduran authorities when he attempted to invade Nicaragua from Honduras), his activity doubtless inspired Miller's dream of an Indian republic in Northern California.

Walker was assuredly a "prince" among men. When he came to California in 1850, he was twenty-six years old. He had graduated from college, achieved a doctoral degree in medicine, studied medicine for a year in Europe after attaining this degree, turned to law, gained admittance to the bar, and edited his own newspaper in New Orleans. He was what Miller aspired to be: a highly educated man, a successful lawyer and writer, a "boy wonder" and a leader of men. Miller, fortunately, did not have Walker's Napoleonic aspirations.

Narration in the first two-thirds of *Life Amongst the Modocs*—the part in which Prince is the dominant character—is chiefly fictional: during 1854 and 1855, Miller had not lived with the Indians nor had he witnessed a massacre of Indians. The last third of the book, relating events from 1855 to 1860, omits his experiences as a miner, herdsman, cook, and college student; and it also exaggerates his participation in the Battle of Castle Crags and in the Pit River massacre and its aftermath and in his outlawry on behalf of the Indians.

He endeavors, wherever possible, to win sympathy and compassion for the Indian. The captured old squaw who carries him, wounded, down from Castle Crags complains: "You have killed all my boys, and burnt up my home." He protests that they had robbed him and Mountain Joe. "No," she replies, "You first robbed us. You drove us from the river. We could not fish, we could not hunt."[21] Having described the needless, terrible butchery of the Pit River Indians, he sadly boasts: "I, and I only, made the bloody expedition a success. I tell this in sorrow. It is a thousand times more to my shame than honour, and I shall never cease to regret it."[22] His subsequent efforts, he says, are devoted to stealing horses and buying arms and ammunition to feed "the half-starved children of the forest." The book, dedicated to "the red men of America," concludes with a promise: "When I die I shall take this book in my hand and hold it up in the Day of Judgment, as a sworn indictment against the rulers of my country for the destruction of this people."[23]

Miller, as hero, emerges fully as an outlaw who endeavors with poor success to be a Robin Hood for the oppressed, decimated Shasta Indians. Like his heroes in song—his Arazonian,

Californian, and Tall Alcalde—he has his Indian mate in lovely Paquita, "tall and lithe and graceful as a mountain lily swayed by the breath of morning." And, after her death, there is another nameless maid who, when goodbyes were said, walks for a way quietly by his side. His valor is unsurpassed. When he learns that "the famous man-killer," Bill Hirst, has accused him of being implicated in the theft of a horse, he takes immediate action:

In Deadwood camp, I entered the main saloon . . . drew a revolver and declared myself chief of the town. I passed from one saloon to another, making this same declaration until toward midnight. While standing with a knot of miners at the bar of Dean's billiard saloon, Hirst entered the far end of the establishment; a tall, splendid fellow, with his hat pushed far back from his brow, flashing eyes, and a pistol in his hand.

Not a sound was heard but the resolute tread of Hirst, as he advanced partly toward me and partly toward the billiard table, while the man at play quietly fell back and left the red and white balls dotting the green cloth.

Those around me sidled away right and left, and I stood alone. Hirst advanced to the table, darting his restless, keen eyes at me every second, and, standing against and leaning over the table, all the time watching me like a cat, he punched the billiard balls savagely with the muzzle of his pistol. He then drew back from the table, tossed his head, whistled something, and moved in my direction.

My hand was on my pistol. The hammer was raised and my finger touched the trigger; but Hirst, without advancing further or saying a word, quietly turned out at the side door and I saw no more of him that night.[24]

In recounting Hirst's later career, Miller admits: "It is but justice to this man to state that he really had lost a horse, taken under my order." What did taking over Deadwood camp for one night prove?—only that he was not afraid of Hirst!

Events leading to Miller's capture and imprisonment in the Shasta City jail are mainly true as he relates them; but the role of Paquita in effecting his escape, their ambush by a platoon of soldiers at the river, Paquita's being caught in a whirlpool and fatally shot—all this leading to her retrieval by the author has no foundation elsewhere in his work. In *Memorie and Rime* he simply states that the Indians "broke open the jail, threw me again on a horse, and such a ride for freedom and fresh air was never before seen." There is no tender death scene here: "Paquita, the child of nature, the sunbeam of the forest, the star that had seen so little of light, lay wrapped in darkness. Paquita lay cold and lifeless in my arms." There is no assertion that "the 'Tale of the Tall Alcalde' was written for her."

Life Amongst the Modocs for many English readers must have been reminiscent of Melville's *Typee*, first published in London twenty-seven years earlier. Both books appeal to the primitivist: instead of Fayaway, there is Paquita. There is the same criticism of the missionary. There is the same description of native customs. While Melville proceeds from autobiography to fiction, Miller proceeds from fiction to half-fiction. Melville's book is of course better planned and better written. Above all, it lacks the constant rapid movement, the carefree optimism, the braggadocio of a Western hero.

III

Miller often reminded hostile Oregonians that he had made Oregon known to the world. Truly, he was himself one of the first striking exhibits, not just of Oregon but of the Wild West. In resplendent attire, tall, and with flowing blonde hair, London so saw him. Later, at his log cabin in Washington, D.C., where he lived for a time apart from his socialite wife, Abbie Leland Miller, the "Poet of the Sierras" was an attraction for almost any tourist of the nation's capital.

For the American East, the poet's harbingers were the dime novels of Western adventure launched by Erastus Beadle in the 1860's. Not that heroes of these thrillers resembled him. While some were indeed "nature's noblemen," many were Eastern aristocrats transplanted and transvested in the West. As such, they did not deign to love Indian women, dress like vaqueros, or for any purpose whatever enter banditry. Those Western heroes of fiction who may be likened to Miller invariably post-date *Songs of the Sierras*. For example, the fictitious Buffalo Bill, first brought to public attention in 1869 by an enterprising romancer, did not begin his world-wide theatricals until the late 1870's. At first no more than "the most daring scout, the best horseman, the best informed guide, and the greatest hunter of the present day," he was by 1878 a folk hero standing between "civilization and savagery, risking his own life to save the lives of others." By 1881, he was for the first time rivaling Miller in his dress; he was described in a story as wearing "a red velvet jacket, white corduroy pants, stuck in handsome top boots, which were armed with heavy gold spurs, and . . . upon his head a gray sombrero, encircled by a gold cord and looped up on the left side with a pin representing a spur."[25]

The popular fictional character most nearly resembling the Miller hero is perhaps Deadwood Dick, a low-born Black Hills bandit and miner, as well as a Don Juan who in his tailored buckskins successfully courts Calamity Jane. Dating from the 1880's, Deadwood Dick, like Buffalo Bill, represents a cheapening of the legendary West through the big business of formula fiction initiated by Beadle, a cheapening that Miller largely ignored.

The dime novel itself fulfilled a dream as ancient as civilized man—the dream of a bliss unencumbered by the apparent artificialities of social conventions. Had Miller published no work other than *Songs of the Sierras* and *Life Amongst the Modocs*, his fame would have been but little diminished, for with these two books he saluted the civilized world as one who from afar had realized the dream. The return salute of the English reviewers was consequently enthusiastic, but in nearly every review there was recognition of artistic limitations. These are not glowing reviews; the critics simply recognized, with deep interest, the promise of a "Heaven-taught genius," the freshness of a wilderness spirit. The London *Spectator* declared: "Mr. Miller's work . . . brings the first-fruits, and the promise of a new soil. It shows a true revival of primitive life in its vigor, simplicity, and occasional rudeness."[26] The *Westminster Review* announced: "We ourselves prefer the roughness of the backwoods of America to all the drawing-room conventionalities of Europe. We prefer Mr. Joaquin Miller's native reed-pipe to any guitar."[27]

Miller's nascent literary star was that of a nineteenth-century Ossian without benefit of translator and editor. He was no Daniel Boone, bringing civilization to the wilderness; he was no Leather-stocking, recognizing the superiority of gentility to frontier rude-ness. Miller was the bard who, outside the West, was himself the symbol and the myth, the promise and the hope of the Great American West. In him emerged the fullness of a new tradition of epic magnitude, combining images of the pathfinder, scout, trapper, miner, pony express rider, homesteader, and herdsman, combining English, Indian, and Spanish elements in the meeting of West with West. He brings a new sympathy for the plight of the red man such as Cooper and Longfellow could never have known. As outlaw, he hears a drummer other than that of the Indian agent or cavalryman of the United States.

Miller's popularity rested not on any substantial artistic ac-complishment but on a passing nostalgic view of the fabulous Western hero as being encompassed or nearly encompassed in himself.

CHAPTER 4

The One Fair Woman

I

IN AN ARTICLE on J. Ross Browne, published in the October 30, 1892, issue of the San Francisco *Call*, Miller makes the following charge: " 'The Innocents Abroad' was as surely born of 'Yusef' as was 'Daisy Miller' born of 'The One Fair Woman.' No, not quite so surely; for on the Pincian Hill, Rome, the same parties, under the same circumstances, at the same time, say exactly the same words." Miller's accusation of plagiarism appears incredible—and *it is false*. Certainly, it does betray his disappointment; for the very novel that in 1876 marked a temporary setback in his own popularity as a writer did quite possibly provide Henry James with a character, a point of view, and several situations for his own early novel, *Daisy Miller*, published two years later. It may be no coincidence that James selected "Miller" as the surname of his central character.

Miller's Mollie Wopsus, like James's Daisy Miller, is an aggressive, inquisitive, ingenuous, irrepressible American girl in pursuit of the attentions of Italian men in Rome. Unlike Daisy, she is a Californian; her speech is louder, more garrulous, and less grammatical: "Well now, you are the worst!" she says upon greeting a friend in Rome. "And when did you come? and where do you go? and where are you now? and where will you be and how have you been?" The next moment she whispers to him: "Do you see those fellows in buttons? All these here? Thick enough to stir 'em with a stick, aren't they? Well, them's my lovers! All them my lovers; just think of it!"[1]

But like Daisy, she will not permit her freedom to be curtailed: "You can't shake me; I come from California, I do, and I know my way about." Daisy's memorable remark to Winterbourne is equally firm: "I have never allowed a gentleman to dictate to me, or to interfere with anything I do." Mollie will not permit unkind words to be spoken about her Italian gallant: "Next thing you'll say something dreadful about Count Paolini, you will! and I won't stand it, I won't!" Daisy simply ignores the counsel that she should not be seen alone with her Italian escort; she will not—and perhaps even cannot—comprehend that he is not a gentleman by European standards. Mollie has one brother, Johnny, a counterpart to Daisy's brother, Randolph. Says Mollie: "He is the worst—bet your life—he is the worst that ever was! Sit down there, Johnny, or you'll drive mother into the tan-ta-rams!"[2] And Mrs. Wopsus is a tearful, fretting mother, who, without mentioning any favorite physician back home, does ask for a doctor in Rome. Like Daisy's mother, she is totally unaware of European mores. She is even pleased and flattered that so many Italian gentlemen are attentive to her daughter.

These "gentlemen" are, of course, fortune-hunters. While Daisy's Giovanelli is of doubtful social position and seeks in Daisy a gratification that may not be wholly monetary, Mollie's Count Paolini is prepared to become a bigamist to acquire Mollie's dowry and inheritance. Mollie, for her part, is eager to marry him before other American girls coming to Rome "crowd the field." His proposal, then, is readily accepted; but Mollie is chagrined about his "being so very particular" about the ceremony: "Well, he don't want any big wedding . . . but I do; bet your life I didn't come all the way from California to be married off like a dummy. Not much, bet your life! that ain't me."[3]

Miller not only maintains throughout his long novel the third-person point of view characteristic of James's fiction but also offers in Murietta the very same type of character found in James's Winterbourne. Both represent their authors; but the characters are not much like Mollie and Daisy. (Of course,

Miller's pen name "Joaquin" is from the name of the Mexican bandit, Joaquin Murietta.) In *The One Fair Woman*, Murietta is an American artist who, like his creator, has been "pronounced . . . a genius of a very high order" and again "denounced . . . as an impostor, a libertine, and a fraud of the very worst stamp."⁴ Murietta even recalls that "he had talked with his sister and his brother when playing on the shores of the Pacific in the shadow of the linden trees of this Eternal City, and had said to them, 'I shall some day see Rome.' And they had said, 'When you see Rome think of us, for we shall then be dead.' "⁵ Miller's elder brother and only sister both died in 1871, two years before his sojourn in Rome.

Winterbourne, of course, has his creator's same interest in women; he studies them, analyzes them, and is fascinated by them. Murietta is less the observer. He carries a romantic vision of the One Fair Woman he met face to face in the most exclusive society of aristocratic London: "Others for others, but she was mine/The one fair woman beneath the sun." He paints her image, and then awaits the day he shall again see her. His reward comes finally after he has rescued the beautiful Countess Edna, "the lady in pink," from rascals who kept her a virtual prisoner in Rome. He meets his *femme ideale* then; she knows all and understands all. "He looked in her face as he spoke; and, holding her hand, drew her close to his breast, and called her his own in a whisper; and she did not shrink away, as he held her hand, but listened to what he chose to say of scattering roses in her path of life now, even to the end."⁶

Murietta's relationship with Mollie is simply fraternal. Not so, Winterbourne's with Daisy. Murietta is racked by Roman fever, not Mollie. Daisy, of course, dies of fever. Mollie's shock upon meeting Count Paolini's wife is temporary (it is Murietta who has led her to the revelation). She does not die; she only reflects sadly: "It is my last night in Rome, or in society at all for a long time."⁷

The Pincian Hill is the scene not of a Mrs. Walker in her carriage determined to sweep Mollie away from "that man," but of Mollie Wopsus in her parents' carriage greeting Murietta.

Says Miller: "She threw out her arms, parasol and all, and caught the artist around the neck as if she were going to smother him or drag him into the carriage." While it is the "cool" Giovanelli on Pincian who stares at women with Daisy's approval, it is Murietta, who in merely conversing with the Countess Edna is startled by Mollie's cry: "Bet your life, here he is, mamma! here he is, making love to the pink princess!"[8]

It is not Murietta (or a Mrs. Costello or a Mrs. Walker) who reflects upon Mollie's conduct; it is the Count! "You know the Count says we American girls are all too fast and loose, and all that, and are liable to get ourselves talked about." Curiously, Mollie, with her one year's education in Paris, agrees with the Count that Americans are "so so very vulgar."[9]

Actually, *The One Fair Woman* cannot be properly called "an international novel," or a novel showing the customs of one country in conflict with those of another. Such conflict is incidental. Moreover, the novel is not "A Study" in character as *Daisy Miller* is; Mollie, in fact, is an extraneous character, if indeed the most memorable character in the work.

The One Fair Woman is a ponderous, improbable mystery story without the foreboding atmosphere and complicated plot of Wilkie Collins' *Moonstone,* published eight years earlier. The first half of Miller's novel is little more than travelogue. The last half recounts the escape of the Countess Edna and her son despite the endeavors of a ring of ruffians who counterfeit money, kidnap a child, betray their fellows, and impersonate monks. The leader of the ring is an old admiral who loves the Countess and wishes to carry her off to America, marry her, and reform. Even Murietta, in pursuit of the One Fair Woman, is susceptible to the charms of the poor Countess: "How beautiful she was! Ah, how more than beautiful! The rose and sea-shell color of her face and neck, the soft baby complexion, the surprise on her face, the old expression of inquiry and longing, the lips pushed out and pouting full and as longing for love, the mouth half-opened as if to ask the way into some great brave heart where she could enter in and sit down and rest, as if some sacred temple."[10] And after Murietta has escorted her to England, she loves none other than the weakly Count, who neglected her and ignored her entreaties to leave Rome and the machinations of the ring!

It is no wonder *The One Fair Woman* never achieved the popularity of *Daisy Miller,* or that the delightful Mollie Wopsus never became the stereotype of the American girl abroad.

Did James use Miller's novel as a source for *Daisy Miller?* One discovered source is Victor Cherbuliez's *Paule Méré.* A source James acknowledges in his correspondence is an anecdote he heard in Rome about "a child of nature and freedom" who, having picked up a prepossessing Italian "of a rather vague identity," was snubbed in the Victorian American society of Rome.[11] Did James recall this anecdote upon reading Miller's novel?

Strangely enough, both James and Miller were residents in Rome early in 1873. While James was there enjoying the companionship of several cultured young women, Miller was sharing the poverty of the denizens of the old Jewish quarter under the Tarpeian Rock. Miller at this time was "miserably poor" though already famous as the Poet of the Sierras. He would not have known about Henry James. More significantly, it is improbable that James would have welcomed the company of the ostentatiously attired Oregonian, whose reputation as a man and writer was held in contempt by many American critics. In James's published letters, there is no mention of Joaquin Miller.

II

Before the publication of *The One Fair Woman* in 1876 Miller had, of course, shown his devotion to The One Fair Woman. She is indeed a veritable quest whether the Far Western hero is at home or abroad. She is the female paragon. She is the Indian maiden in *Songs of the Sierras* and the Amazon Queen in *Songs of the Sun-lands.* She is dusky Ina in *The Ship in the Desert*— the Ina who is called "this one fair woman of the world":

> I only saw her as she pass'd—
> A great, sad beauty, in whose eyes
> Lay all the loves of Paradise.[12]

After the nameless beauty and the Countess Edna in *The One Fair Woman*, she is Adora in *The Baroness of New York* (1877):

> A maiden by the river's brink,
> Stood fair to see as you can think,
> As tall as tules at her feet.
> As fair as flowers in her hair,
> As sweet as flowers over-sweet.
> As fair as wood-nymph, more than fair.
> How beautiful she was! How wild!
> How pure as water-plant, this child—
> This one wild child of nature here
> Grown tall in shadows. And how near
> To God, where no man stood between
> Her eyes and scenes no man hath seen.

And again:

> How beautiful! How proud and free!
> How more than Greek or Tuscan she
> In full development. Her mouth
> Was majesty itself. Give me
> A mouth as warm as summer south—
> A great, Greek mouth, for through this gate
> Man first must pass to love's estate.[13]

She is Lilian in *The Songs of Italy* (1878):

> Her name is as language; and when I know
> Nor name nor type to give utterance to
> My grandest conception of woman, she
> Stands up in my soul, calm, silently,
> And fills the blank with her own sweet name.[14]

She is Hattie Lane in *The Destruction of Gotham* (1886), "the one fair woman forever." She is the Indian maid in "The Sea of Fire" (1887).

She is beautiful. She is loving. She is no critic. According to Miller, "When woman arises and asserts herself, as the sharp-tongued, thin-lipped puritaness proposes, and is no longer dependent, man's arm will no longer be reached as a shield. . . .

Whenever woman succeeds in making herself a soldier she must fight."[15] (Views of this sort he had expressed long before—in debate in 1854 at West Point School.) Woman exists only for love, it would seem, and on this subject Miller is most prolific. In "With Walker in Nicaragua," for instance, he declares:

> Love well who will, love well who can,
> But love, be loved, for God is love;
> Love pure, like cherubim above;
> Love maids, and hate not any man.

And again the same *carpe diem* theme:

> Love while 'tis day; night cometh soon,
> Wherein no man or maiden may;
> Love in the strong young prime of day;
> Drink drink with love in the red noon,
> Red noon of love and life and sun;
> Walk in love's light as in sunshine;
> Drink in that sun as drinking wine;
> Drink swift, nor question any one;
> For loves change sure as man or moon,
> And wane like warm full days of June.[16]

Miller held that love with a woman is sacred whether within or without marriage. Love is pure and so is the beloved. Let no man—or woman—cast a stone:

> Doth priest know aught
> Of sign, or holy unction brought
> From over seas, that ever can
> Make man love maid or maid love man
> One whit the more, one bit the less,
> For all his mummeries to bless?
> Yea, all his blessings or his ban?[17]

The critic in the London *Spectator,* in reviewing *Songs of the Sierras,* noted perceptively: "Until the Byronic glamour is removed from his eyes, he has no chance of really seeing a woman."[18] Certainly, Miller viewed woman glamorously but without Byron's insight into a woman's feelings. He saw woman as did Théophile Gautier, but without Gautier's elaborate, decorative trappings. He saw woman as did Oscar Wilde, who said of the face of their mutual friend, the actress Lily Langtry: "Pure Greek it is, with the grave low forehead, the exquisitely arched brow; the noble chiselling of the mouth, shaped as if it were the mouthpiece of an instrument of music; the supreme and splendid curve of the cheek; the augustly pillared throat which bears it all: it is Greek because the lines which compose it are so definite and so strong, and yet so exquisitely harmonized that the effect is one of simple loveliness purely: Greek, because its essence and its quality, as is the quality of music and of architecture, is that of beauty based on absolutely mathematical laws."[19] Miller also had described Lily Langtry—or so he told her. She is The One Fair Woman in his books published in the mid-1870's.

Miller was ever gallant, ever appreciative of young women friends whom he entreated to visit him on his hillside acres above Oakland, California. They came, often with their mothers but rarely with their husbands. He had guest cabins for them (these he had built himself) and sometimes greeted them with a favorite compliment. Some of Miller's women friends in California saw him week by week, over a period of years, at his home on the hillside. Presumably they were satisfied by his limited tribute—not to their minds but to their charms. A witness describes the greeting that Miller, then an elderly man, gave Lily Langtry in California: "When Mrs. Langtry appeared, robed with the perfection of taste that has helped make her name world-famed, Joaquin advanced to meet her, led by Mrs. Flower. As the introduction took place, Joaquin seemed not to notice the proffered hand of Mrs. Langtry, but, rapidly raising both hands to his sombrero, took hold of it and dexterously showered upon the astonished lady a wealth of beautiful rose leaves, at the same time jerking out in his most jerky fashion, 'the tribute of the California roses to Jersey Lily.' "[20]

His preoccupation with The One Fair Woman continued

throughout his life. As late as "The Song of Creation" (1903), she reappears in a chant as rhythmic, repetitive, and vigorous as any he ever wrote. Here, however, she is not as limited as her many predecessors. To begin with, she is married—and appreciated as a wife:

> Why, what a glorious thing to view!
> Each morn a maiden at your side,
> The one fair woman, maid and bride.[21]

Unlike her predecessors, she is a devoted mother: she not only "loves her spouse most ardently" but also, as Miller puts it tritely, "loves to fold the little frock." Even in the most passionate of scenes, her humor suggests character:

> He turned, he caught her suddenly
> And instant wrapped her close within;
> Then down the stairs and back and out
> Beneath the blossomed Nippon tree—
> Against the tree he pressed her form,
> He was so warm, so very warm—
> He held her close as close could be
> Against the blossomed cherry tree.
>
> He held with all his might and main—
> Held her so hard she shook the tree. . . .
> She laughed such low, sweet laugh, and said,
> The while she raised her pretty head,
> "Please, please, be gentle good to me,
> And please don't hurt the cherry tree."[22]

Her hero also loves her with gentle, lasting care:

> All voiceless, noiseless, tenderly
> He pressed beside her, took her hand—
> He took her from the leaning moon,
> And far beyond the amber sea,
> They sailed the seas of afternoon—
> The far, still seas, so grandly grand,
> Until they came to babyland.[23]

He is not a Western hero but a hero of all mankind, a worthy son of Biblical "giants in the land." Unconquerable youth is his hallmark:

> Why, man, each well-born man was born
> To dwell in everlasting morn,
> To top the mountain as a tower,
> A thousand years of pride and power;
> To face the four winds with the face
> Of youth until full length he lies—
> Still God-like, even as he dies.[24]

The procreative tie, youth until death, the divinity of man—these are new dimensions for The One Fair Woman at the outset of the twentieth century, "this glorious, shining, new-born age."

And yet, to the end, Miller denies her the gift of intellect. Like Milton's Eve, she sees only the man and their life ahead: "He looked to heaven, God; but she/Saw only his face and the sea."[25]

CHAPTER 5

The Writer's Craft

I

IN *Songs of the Sierras,* Miller confessed, "Poetry with me is a passion that defies reason." And, to be sure, he does not reason in his poetry. He simply narrates, describes, affirms, and reaffirms. In his most famous poem, "Columbus," published in *Songs of the Soul* (1896), he does succeed in presenting effectively a series of scenes in five stanzas, all leading to the discovery of a light—and a new world:

> Behind him lay the gray Azores,
> Behind the Gates of Hercules;
> Before him not the ghost of shores;
> Before him only shoreless seas.
> The good mate said: "Now must we pray,
> For lo? the very stars are gone,
> Brave Adm'r'l speak; what shall I say?"
> "Why, say: 'Sail on! sail on! and on!'"
>
> "My men grow mutinous day by day;
> My men grow ghastly, wan and weak."
> The stout mate thought of home; a spray
> Of salt wave washed his swarthy cheek.
> "What shall I say, brave Adm'r'l, say,
> If we sight naught but seas at dawn?"
> "Why, you shall say at break of day:
> 'Sail on! sail on! sail on! and on!'"

They sailed and sailed, as winds might blow,
    Until at last the blanched mate said:
"Why, not now even God would know
    Should I and all my men fall dead.
These very winds forget their way,
    For God from these dread seas is gone.
Now speak, brave Adm'r'l, speak and say—"
    He said: "Sail on! sail on! and on!"

They sailed. They sailed. Then spake the mate:
    "This mad sea shows his teeth tonight.
He curls his lip, he lies in wait,
    He lifts his teeth, as if to bite!
Brave Adm'r'l, say but one good word:
    What shall we do when hope is gone?"
The words leapt like a leaping sword:
    "Sail on! sail on! sail on! and on!"

Then pale and worn, he paced his deck,
    And peered through darkness. Ah, that night
Of all dark nights! And then a speck—
    A light! A light! At last a light!
It grew, a starlit flag unfurled!
    It grew to be Time's burst of dawn.
He gained a world; he gave that world
    Its grandest lesson: "On! sail on!"[1]

Unfortunately, the mate's view of Columbus prevails: the
Columbus of the refrain who in his obsession is unreasonable,
unfeeling, and insane. "Sail on! sail on! and on!" he says in the
face of mutiny and death when, as the mate believes, God—and
hope—are gone. At the end, Miller declares that the "grandest
lesson" Columbus gave the world is "On! sail on!" Yet it must
be said that while Columbus, with his "on! sail on!" *ad nauseam*,
may be the personification of the very commonplace lesson,
"Don't give up," his unvarying affirmation and reaffirmation
have made this poem very susceptible to parody in the schools
of a generation or two ago in which it was recited. Indeed, the
suspicion is very strong that Miller's Columbus would not have

reached the New World at all: the good mate and his men would have pitched him overboard halfway across the Atlantic.

In a note appended to "Columbus" in the collected *Poems* Miller declares that it is not the best American poem: "It is far from that; even I have done better; too much like a chorus. 'The Passing of Tennyson' is better. 'The Missouri' better still." For ready comparison Miller placed these after "Columbus" in the *Poems*.

Also from *Songs of the Soul*, "The Passing of Tennyson" mourns a procession of great British and American poets who died one after the other—Robert Browning, 1889; James Russell Lowell, 1891; and Walt Whitman and John Greenleaf Whittier, 1892, the year of Tennyson's death.

> My kingly kinsmen, kings of thought,
>   I hear your gathered symphonies,
> Such nights as when the world is not,
>   And great stars chorus through my trees.
>
>   ✿   ✿   ✿   ✿   ✿   ✿   ✿
>
> We knew it, as God's prophets knew;
>   We knew it, as mute red men know,
> When Mars leapt searching heaven through
>   With flaming torch, that he must go.
> Then Browning, he who knew the stars,
> Stood forth and faced insatiate Mars.
>
> Then up from Cambridge rose and turned
>   Sweet Lowell from his Druid trees—
> Turned where the great star blazed and burned,
>   As if his own soul might appease.
> Yet on and on through all the stars
> Still searched and searched insatiate Mars.
>
> Then staunch Walt Whitman saw and knew;
>   Forgetful of his "Leaves of Grass,"
> He heard his "Drum Taps," and God drew
>   His great soul through the shining pass,
> Made light, made bright by burnished stars;
> Made scintillant from flaming Mars.

Then soft-voiced Whittier was heard
   To cease; was heard to sing no more,
As you have heard some sweetest bird
   The more because its song is o'er.
Yet brighter up the street of stars
Still blazed and burned and beckoned Mars.

And then the king came; king of thought,
   King David with his harp and crown. . . .
How wisely well the gods had wrought
   That these had gone and sat them down
To wait and welcome 'mid the stars
All silent in the light of Mars.

     *   *   *   *   *   *   *

All silent. . . . So, he lies in state. . . .
   Our redwoods drip and drip with rain. . . .
Against our rock-locked Golden Gate
   We hear the great sad, sobbing main,
But silent all. . . . He passed the stars
That year the whole world turned to Mars.[2]

Some dignity does emerge in the poem. Poets in heaven wait with King David, the greatest singer of them all; but all are silent now as Tennyson completes the death-claiming quest of "insatiate" Mars. Apart from the trite "great sad, sobbing main," the concluding stanza offers appropriately restrained emotion even though it appears that "the whole world," or all great poets, are being taken.

Miller, however, makes enormous sacrifices to preserve his unvarying iambic tetrameter and his rhymes. "Such nights as when the world is not" is meaningless but does supply a needed rhyme in *not*. "We knew it" at the beginning of the first line of the second stanza is repeated at the beginning of the second, but what "we knew" is not known. Indeed, the reader forgets that he needs to know anything by the end of the fourth line where the answer abruptly and awkwardly appears. In the third stanza the poet expediently makes *appease* intransitive; a rhyme for *trees* is thus provided while the reader is tripped poetically in supplying his own *it*. In the fourth stanza the reader is informed that "Whittier was heard/To cease." But apparently, with *cease,* Miller felt he had extended beyond his reader's vocabulary; for he adds "was heard to sing no more"—or was he reaching hard to match the poetic contraction *o'er?*

And so it goes. One is not surprised that the fifth stanza has its own catastrophe in "How wisely well the gods had wrought/ That these had gone and sat them down." Just what the gods had *wrought* is a mystery; indeed, it is a greater mystery what *gods* are doing in a poem where God's prophets prophesy, where God (or Mars?) directs Whitman, and where in the same stanza King David with harp and crown has just arrived. *These* is also mystifying until its antecedent is found—in the first stanza: Poor dead poets. They undoubtedly feel "sat down" rather hard. That Mars overlooked Joaquin Miller for yet twenty-one years is surely a tribute to them.

"The Missouri" is a far better poem. The river is presented not as the trapper, miner, or rancher knew it in detail; it is generalized and personified—made symbolic of the magnitude and power of the West: buffalo—millions of them, gold "in cradlefuls," and mountaintops of endlessly huge variety. Such is the setting of the source and the range of the great river.

> Where ranged thy black-maned, woolly bulls
> By millions, fat and unafraid;
> Where gold, unclaimed in cradlefuls,
> Slept 'mid the grass roots, gorge, and glade;
> Where peaks companioned with the stars,
> And propped the blue with shining white,
> With massive silver beams and bars,
> With copper bastions, height on height—
> There wast thou born, O lord of strength!
> O yellow lion, leap and length
> Of arm from out an Arctic chine
> To far, fair Mexic seas are thine!
>
> What colors? Copper, silver, gold
> With sudden sweep and fury blent,
> Enwound, unwound, inrolled, unrolled,
> Mad molder of the continent!

What whirlpools and what choking cries
    From out the concave swirl and sweep
As when some god cries out and dies
    Ten fathoms down thy tawny deep!
Yet on, right on, no time for death,
No time to gasp a second breath!
You plow a pathway through the main
To Morro's castle, Cuba's plain.

Hoar sire of hot, sweet Cuban seas,
    Gray father of the continent,
Fierce fashioner of destinies,
    Of states thou hast upreared or rent,
Thou knowst no limit; seas turn back,
    Bent, broken from the shaggy shore;
But thou, in thy resistless track,
    Art lord and master evermore.
Missouri, surge and sing and sweep!
Missouri, master of the deep,
From snow-reared Rockies to the sea
Sweep on, sweep on eternally![3]

Highly alliterative and repetitive in word and phrase, the ex-clamatory verse falters occasionally. The promising metaphor, "O yellow lion," gives way to "leap and length/Of arm from out an Arctic chine," a most ungainly movement of words and certainly unworthy of a yellow-lion river. More reprehensible is the inane comparison of the sound of the "concave swirl and sweep" to the cry of a god dying under the flood: who is this god—and who has heard him? In the same passage it is also un-clear why the Missouri should "gasp a second breath." Although "peaks companioned with the stars,/And propped the blue with shining white" is magnificent expression, it is offset by the con-ventional "gorge and glade," "hoar sire," and "lord and master." Even "The Missouri," one of Miller's best poems, does not bear close reading.

    This failure to analyze and to perceive through analysis is the shortcoming that has doubtless prevented Miller, as a popular poet, from becoming a truly great one. His lesser faults are legion. His unidiomatic English and his miserable rhymes are mainly attributable to haste in writing and to inadequate revision. Just how disastrous these can be in some of his otherwise more successful poems can be shown all too readily. An example is this couplet in "With Walker in Nicaragua":

> I sought to know no more than this
> Of history of him or his.

Or, from the same poem:

> So much the leaded dice of war
> Do make or mar of character.[4]

Less awkward than these unidiomatic verses is "from off the scene," the final, superfluous fill-in phrase for the sake of rhyme in an otherwise impressive passage from "Adios":

> Could I but teach man to believe—
> Could I but make small men to grow,
> To break frail spider-webs that weave
> About their thews and bind them low;
> Could I but sing one song and slay
> Grim Doubt; I then could go my way
> In tranquil silence, glad, serene,
> And satisfied, from off the scene.[5]

Melodrama can become downright insufferable. In "The Tale of the Tall Alcalde," the villain is a "tawny advocate" who cries:

> "'Tis the renegade of the red McCloud
> Seize him, hasten you, hold him fast,
> Revenge is sweet—it is mine at last!"[6]

Happily, the last two verses were excised from the 1910 revision of the poem.

Unimaginative, unmotivated, and inexplicable actions within his narrative are frequent. In *The Baroness of New York*, Doughal, a captain who deserts Adora to seek wealth and fame, precedes Sir Francis, who as "the fairest of men" can only be Miller himself. Re-enter Doughal, who reclaims the lady. He now has titles she will not despise, for now (and without explanation) he is Lord Adair! Whatever these events represent in the friendship of Miller and Lily Langtry, in the poem Adora, Sir Francis—and the reader—are all betrayed: the rascal is rewarded.

Miller's devotion to Byron was a severe handicap from which he extricated himself only with great difficulty toward the end of his writing career. Indeed, his early verse is often slavishly imitative of Byron's Eastern tales and lyrics, not of Byron's social satire in *Don Juan* or satirical revenge in "English Bards and Scotch Reviewers." Miller borrowed Byron's style, characters, and situations—Byron's verse tale written in iambic pentameter, with repeated use of a word like *paynim;* Byron's proud, passionate, defiant outcast hero removed to a Western setting; and Byron's story in early poems such as "Benoni" (cf. "Prisoner of Chillon") and "Joaquin" (cf. *The Island,* Canto IV). In style, Miller was never Byron's equal. His heroes—unlike Byron's—are not persistently moody, and his heroines come rarely from Byron at all. His plots are no credit to Byron—action is usually unmotivated, obscure, unbelievable.

In revising his poems shortly before his death, Miller strove for independence of expression; he changed a borrowing like *paynim* to *Northmen,* and he eliminated descriptive passages and intrusive reflections. Miss Gabriella Brendemuhl, in her unpublished dissertation, "Joaquin Miller's Indebtedness to Byron," has prepared the following table indicating the extent to which Miller reduced nine of ten poems in the American edition of *Songs of the Sierras:*

Poem	1871	1910
Arazonian	19 (pages)	14 (pages)
Californian	39	11
The Last Taschastas	18	12
Ina	63	18
The Tale of the Tall Alcalde	44	29
Kit Carson's Ride	8	5
Burns and Byron	9	7
Myrrh	6	4
Even So	20	10
With Walker in Nicaragua	38	54

Even more drastic revision is seen in the reduction of *The Baroness of New York* (231 pages) to "The Sea of Fire" (46 pages) in *Songs of the Mexican Seas.*

Most significant in these revisions is the departure from literary models—from Browning's "How They Brought the Good News from Ghent to Aix," in cutting the last fifty-six lines of "Kit Carson's Ride" to merely three, in deleting the confession scene in "Joaquin" so similar to one in Byron's *The Giaour,* and in discarding altogether Byronic social satire in Part II, "On Fifth Avenue," of *The Baroness of New York* and in retaining but a section of Part I with a new (if melodramatic) conclusion freed from classical allusions and an Eastern setting.[7]

Although Miller does slavishly imitate Byron and other nineteenth-century British poets in much of his early poetry, he does at times show an original distinctive style that is characterized by highly alliterative verses with repetition of certain words on which the chant turns back upon itself before moving forward again. The rapid, rocking movement is developed by balanced verses with the caesura appearing regularly in the middle of each verse. The "songs" or chants are not inappropriate to the primitive life of the hero they celebrate, removed from reality as he is. When the poet wearied of writing of his hero at home in the West and took him abroad or into society, he also changed his poetic style. Sometimes, as in "For Pauline" in *Songs of Italy,* his refrain recalls a Jonsonian love song:

> Love me, love, but breathe it low,
> Soft as summer weather;
> If you love me, tell me so,
>   As we sit together,
> Sweet and still as roses blow:
> Love me, love, but breathe it low.[8]

Equally delightful, even in their poignancy, are these lines:

> Some levelled hills, a wall, a dome
> That lords its gilded arch and lies,
> While at its base a beggar cries
> For bread, and dies,—and that is Rome.[9]

Pleasantly reminiscent of Swinburne, another nineteenth-century English poet whom Miller sometimes imitated excessively,[10] are sibilants in "Those Perilous Spanish Eyes":

> Some fragrant trees,
> Some flower-sown seas
> Where boats go up and down,
> And a sense of rest
> To the tired breast
> In this beauteous Aztec town.[11]

Whether in Europe, in the American East or the West, Miller ignored the distinguishing features of the landscape and of men. Even Rome, with its "levelled hills" and "gilded arch," could be one of many places; and the beggar could be one of many such men. In poetry Miller does not linger over wretchedness; it is enough to note it and to sing on—to be "the bravest old hero" whose outlook is expressed in the title of the poem, "The World Is a Better World," and in the poem itself:

> Aye, the world is a better old world today!
> And a great good mother this earth of ours;
> Her white tomorrows are a white stairway
> To lead us up to the far star flowers—
> The spiral tomorrows that one by one
> We climb and we climb in the face of the sun.
>
> Aye, the world is a braver old world today!
> For many a hero dares bear with wrong—
> Will laugh at wrong and will turn away;
> Will whistle it down the wind with a song—
> Dares slay the wrong with his splendid scorn!
> The bravest old hero that ever was born![12]

The hero, of course, is once again none other than Joaquin Miller, poet.

Generally, his best poems are descriptive rather than narrative, and his best descriptive verses are metaphorical. In "The Sea of Fire," the Madonna-like Indian maid is likened to the moon:

> She drew
> Men upward as a moon of spring
> High wheeling, vast, and bosom-full,
> Half-clad in clouds and white as wool,
> Draws all the strong seas following.[13]

In "The American Ocean," the setting sun becomes a wounded swan:

> Aye, day is done, the dying sun
> Sinks wounded unto death tonight;
> A great hurt swan, he sinks to rest,
> His wings all crimson, blood his breast!
> With wide, low wings, reached left and right,
> He sings, and night and swan are one—
> One huge, black swan of Helicon.[14]

Such images are more frequently to be found in the later poetry. Beginning comparatively late in his career as a poet (he was already thirty-four years of age when his *Songs of the Sierras* was published), he learned eventually to write with deliberate care, to rewrite and revise. Unfortunately, by the late 1880's and 1890's he had exhausted favorite themes, and there remained for him only the composing of an occasional new poem or the refashioning of an old one.

Though he wrote more books of verse than prose, he once declared, "I am sure I never had much idea of my verses."[15] He was also no critic of his own work or of others'. He was an appreciator; he was a celebrator. He placed a wreath of laurel on the grave of Byron. He paid tribute to numerous nineteenth-century British poets in articles written for San Francisco newspapers. He raised monuments to Pope and Browning on his Oakland hills. "Burns and Byron" and "The Passing of Tennyson" are poems of earnest praise: *Burns,* "another name for song"; *Byron,* "a solitary light"; and *Tennyson,* "he passed the stars."

What is poetry? In *Memorie and Rime* Miller's reply is that "life is poetry, because life is beauty, and the world is one vast unwritten poem." It would follow, evidently, that poetry is beauty —or is it only unwritten poetry? Elsewhere in the same essay he says that poetry is "the love of the beautiful" and that the poet's message should be the text: "And God saw everything that He had made, and, behold, it was very good." It is what God, not man, has made that is very good. The noble savages, "they are the truest lovers of a beautiful world—these negroes with their tranquil natures, the Indians with their deep insight, their silent dignity, and their awful reverence for the God of Nature. They are content with the world." Their opposites are "a race of vulgar and suspicious money-getting merchants, with laws . . . of bankruptcy."[16]

Miller, to be sure, had not appreciated the Negro during the Civil War; but, shortly afterward and through his elder brother John, he had abandoned his pro-slavery views. In his journal for 1870-71, published in *Memorie and Rime,* he offers an explanation: "But when the war came, and the armies went down desolating the South, then, with that fatality that has always followed me for getting on the wrong side, siding with the weak, I forgot my pity for the one [the Negro] in my larger pity for the other."[17] Paquita is Indian; Ina, Negro: Miller celebrated both races through their women. One must only protest that Miller had created them, not God, who would have given them life.

But perhaps one should not expect "life" in a utopian primitivism, where all nature's children are to enjoy forever the beauty and passion with which God endowed them. Miller saw the earth as a not-quite-fallen Eden: the evil exploiter is in the Garden; nature's child, though hurt, is incorruptible. The hated, homeless Jew is to be saved from the Russian bear.[18] The Cuban slave is to be freed from the fetters of his Spanish master.[19] The poor Boer farmer is wrongly assaulted by an imperialist power.[20] Miller is not a Columbus discovering a new world; he is a relentless romantic seeking to re-create a very old world that never existed. The dream of an Indian republic at Mount Shasta is too small a dream; simple folk deserve Mount Shastas everywhere.

What can be said, finally, about Miller the poet? None of the twelve major books of his poetry has been reprinted during the past several decades; but he himself spent his last years selecting and revising poems to appear in six volumes. More than half his poetry was published in the 1870's. The scattered volumes of later years are shorter and not particularly noteworthy. In these he reprints earlier poems: he returns to Civil War subjects, to description of the Pacific coasts, and to The One Fair Woman and love. A versifier of noble, elemental feelings, he is a moralist who usually lacks precision, subtlety, and originality. Most importantly, he is no thinker, no philosopher; and he is, therefore, in the most elevated conception of the word—no poet.

II

Compared to his poetry, his prose published in book form is meager, even though he claimed to prefer writing prose. In addition to *Life Amongst the Modocs, The One Fair Woman,* and *Memorie and Rime* (this last having more "memorie" than rime), his most important prose includes *First Fam'lies in the Sierras* (1875), a Bret Harte kind of story: there is the mining camp (the Forks) with its saloon (the Howling Wilderness); its inseparable partners (Sandy and Limber Tim); Chinaman (Washee-Washee); worn-out prostitutes with compassionate hearts (Bunkerhill and Captain Tommy); and a regular Sunday funeral—not, says Miller, "because these bad women were there, but because the good women were not there." Then, like Bret Harte, the good woman (the Widow) comes and transforms the community. The men, made gentler, no longer appear naked to the waist on a Sunday washday; while their only shirt is drying, they either stay in bed or button a coat up all the way to the chin. The Widow cures Deboon of his illness and Washee-Washee of his clever thefts. Her two chief suitors are Sandy and the Parson (not an actual "gospel sharp" but one so called because of his cursing "like a cannon ball, and red hot too"). They become fierce rivals.

Though inarticulate, Sandy becomes the Western hero in a tavern scene that has become the stock-in-trade in nearly every "Western" since Owen Wister's *Virginian*. While the two barkeepers pile sand-bags behind the counter, the Parson takes a seat and faces the door. Expectant onlookers, very careful to leave a broad path between the door and the Parson, become impatient. There are whisperings that Sandy "Hasn't got the soul of a chicken!" that he is "Caved in at last!" and "Gone down in his boots!" and "Busted in the snapper!" and "Lost his grip," and "Don't dare show his hand." Sandy enters:

Neither of Sandy's hands were visible; but, as the Parson took a few steps forward, and partly drew his hand from his pocket, Sandy's right one came up like a steel spring, and the ugly black muzzle of a six-shooter was in the Parson's face.

Still he advanced, till his face almost touched the muzzle of the pistol. He seemed not to see it, or to have the least perception of his danger. . . .

"Sandy . . . I am going away."[21]

The Judge, a magistrate who can speak of little else than "the glorious climate of Californy," must now perform a marriage ceremony. What follows is a humor straight out of *Roughing It:*

He stood there trying hard to begin. He could hear the men breathe. The pretty little woman was troubled too. . . .

"Do you solemnly swear?"

The Judge had jerked himself together with an effort that made his joints fairly rattle. He hoisted his right hand in the air as he said this, and, having once broken ground, he went on—"Do you solemnly swear to love, and honour, and obey?"

It was very painful. . . . At last the Judge revived, and began again in a voice that was full of desperation.

"Do you solemnly swear to love, and protect, and honour, and obey, till death do you part; and——"

Here the voice fell down low, lower, and the Judge was again floundering in water. Then his head went under utterly. Then he rose, and "Now I lay me down to sleep" rolled tremulously through the silent room from the lips of the Judge. Then again the head went under water, then it rose up again, and there was something like "Twinkle, twinkle, little star." Then the voice died again, the head was under water. Then it rose again, and the head went up high in air, and the voice was loud and resolute, and the man rose on his tiptoes, and beginning with—"When in the course of human events," he went on in a deep and splendid tone with the Declaration of Independence, to the very teeth of tyrannical King George, and then bringing his hand down emphatically on the gambling table that stood to his right, said loud, and clear, and resolute, and authoritatively, as he tilted forward on his toes, "So help you God, and I pronounce you man and wife."[22]

Sandy must now face his partner, Limber Tim, and the Mark Twain humor continues: "It was a moment of terrible embarrassment. When an Englishman is embarrassed he takes snuff; when a Yankee is embarrassed, he whips out a jackknife and falls to whittling anything he can find, not excepting the ends of his fingers; but a true Californian of the Sierras jerks his head at the boys, heads straight up to the bar, knocks his knuckles on the board, winks at the bartender, pecks his nose at his favorite bottle, fills to the brim, nods his head down the line of the left, then to the right, hoists his Poison, throws back his head, and then falls back wiping his mouth with the back of his hand, quite recovered from his confusion."[23]

After the marriage, the story becomes a plagiarism of Harte's "The Luck of Roaring Camp." The Widow gives birth to a baby, and the miners react just as the miners in Harte's story when they first see the baby Luck:

"Well ef that ain't the littlest!"
"Is that all the big they is?"
"Ain't mor'n a half-pint! is it, Gopher?"
"Well! don't think Sandy hardly got his first planting, did he, Pike?"
"Well, that bangs me all hollow!"
"Dang my cats if it's bigger nor my thumb!"

Harte's miners comment as follows:

"Is that him?"
"Mighty small specimen."
"Hasn't mor'n got the color."
"He rastled with my finger . . . the d----d little cuss!"

Harte's good will to Joaquin Miller had cooled when the "Poet of the Sierras" was being lionized in London. The two men ignored each other after the publication of *First Fam'lies*. Even as late as 1892, Miller, in writing a series of essays on California writers for the San Francisco *Call*, omitted the most important one—Bret Harte.

Washee-Washee follows precisely the Heathen Chinee, the type Bret Harte created in "Plain Language from Truthful James." Unlike Mark Twain, who also favored the underdog, Miller did not sympathize with the Chinese. He believed that the railroad construction had brought the worst class of Chinese to America. In the dramatic version of *First Fam'lies*, retitled *The Danites in the Sierras*, he presents the Mormons unfavorably (as did Mark Twain also in *Roughing It*); but Miller later regretted his dark portrayal of a persecuted people whom he no longer could regard as evil.

Although imitative of both Harte and Twain, *First Fam'lies* is still today Miller's most attractive tale. The 151 pages of the first edition published in London could easily have been reduced to half that number had Miller taken care to tighten the story by eliminating repetition, contradiction, and unnecessarily long suspense. (Twenty-three pages pass between the news of the Widow's mysterious and seemingly desperate illness and the revelation of her pregnancy.) But intrusive author reflections are here both briefer and less frequent than in *Life Amongst the Modocs*, where Miller digressed on such subjects as the use of the first person, the suffragette movement, and the evils of gold and warfare.

The last three books of prose fiction—all published in the 1880's—are, artistically, very disappointing. *Shadows of Shasta* (1881) is sheer propaganda on behalf of the Indian, without the attractive social settings of Helen Hunt Jackson's *Ramona*, published three years later and succeeding far better than Miller's book in winning support for recognition of the rights of the Indians. In an introduction Miller declares that his story is told because he himself had seen Indians, women and children chained together, being led down from the Sierras to a reservation where the agent's income was dependent upon the number of Indians under his care. The story is about an Indian youth, John Logan, a speaker of surprisingly refined English, whose home is confiscated and whose very person is sought by two evil Indian agents. After being harbored by two Indian waifs, a boy and girl protected by the lonely miner called Forty-nine, John is captured; he languishes and dies on a reservation where his two little friends die with him. Forty-nine is there too. The sentiment becomes predictably mawkish: "Forty-nine, father! Let me call you father; may I? I never had any father but you." And to the dying girl's entreaty he replies: "Yes, yes, call me father . . . do call me father, for of all the world, I have only you to love and live for."[24] Forty-nine then buries the dead girl by his cabin in the Sierras.

Miller does not share in *Shadows of Shasta*, as he does in *Life Amongst the Modocs*, his insight into Indian custom and lore; nor does he offer much perspective concerning the plight of California's Indians. He never alludes to the comparatively humane attitude of Spanish Americans who christianized Indians throughout Central and Southern California; they recognized that an Indian had a soul to be saved. By contrast, the invasion of thousands of Anglo-American miners into Northern California during the Gold Rush resulted in the killing of Indians as if they were wild animals. Paquita's brothers had spoken truly: "If you bring men and dig gold here, we must all die." Yet in California no reservation was ever established, even though Modocs were placed in the Klamath Reservation in Oregon. Influential Californians, from Yreka to Sacramento, sought relief for the Indians. Miller's was not the only voice, but his was widely heard.

The character Forty-nine reappears in *'49: The Gold-Seeker of the Sierras* (1884), where his story is told more fully. Forty-nine is one Charlie Devine, who left his wife and child to cross the plains with the promise to return in one year with gold. Once in the gold fields, his destitution prevents his return. Gold fever spurs him to work deeply into his mine for years after his arrival. A series of incredible coincidences conclude in a happy ending: Forty-nine's son (now a young man) arrives and becomes his father's partner, but neither realizes the other's identity. When Forty-nine sees that the girl he has reared is attracted to the boy, he contemplates killing him; but he is soon stunned by a song the boy sings; it is the special song of his own wife. Forty-nine then decides to withhold his discovery from the boy until gold is found in the mine. When the boy is later charged with murder by the Vigilantes, his mother arrives. Forty-nine takes his place when execution without trial is to occur, but at the last minute he is recognized despite the black shroud. Mean-time, the actual murderer is caught; gold is found in Forty-nine's mine; and the girl learns that she is an heiress lost in the Moun-tain Meadow Massacre.

The Destruction of Gotham (1886) begins somewhat as Stephen Crane's *Maggie* ends: a girl adrift walks endlessly down streets of New York without means and without relief. Neither is really "a girl of the streets": Dottie Lane flees from prostitu-tion; Maggie invites it unsuccessfully. Unlike Maggie, who "blossomed in a mud puddle" in a city tenement district, Dottie enters innocently from the hinterland. Unlike Crane, whose high-ly selective scenes in *Maggie* are presented dispassionately, Mil-ler damns New York with all the certainty of the prophet Amos: "The great city lies trembling, panting, quivering in her wild, white heat of intoxication, excitement, madness—drunken and devilish pursuits of power, pleasure, and gold."[25] The agent of the Devil is the procuress, "terrible, grinning creature," whose patient pursuit of Dottie, block after block, can lead only to "the reward." The Devil is the financier, whom Miller views dis-tantly without discrimination: "Look at the great gamblers, the big, red-faced men, with their big, red fists clutching tight and close to their millions upon millions. These are the men who maintain her in her trade—great spiders, in their webs of wire and railroad tracks, waiting to devour the body and soul she brings. Destroy these, and you destroy her."[26] Dottie is the vehicle of the author's wrath. The novel is the baleful, back-ward look of one who never returned to the city—of one who there played the devil himself and lost a small fortune when tricked (or given bad advice) by none other than Jay Gould.[27]

Clearly, Miller's forte is not fiction: at best his characters are either appealing caricatures of eccentric miners or impressive representations of the Western hero. When he leaves the West and the Westerner, as he does in *The Destruction of Gotham,* he loses a grand setting, a noble hero, and a deserving cause. He does, however, excel in autobiography: in *Memorie and Rime* and in the autobiographical introduction to the collected poems, his manner is straightforward, his diction simple, his meanings instantly clear. At times one detects overtones of the Bible or of the orator; and on every page is detected the author's pride in valiant action, his treasuring of the remembrance of his deeds. Unfortunately, *Memorie and Rime* is a mere miscellany of autobiographical pieces, and the introduction to the collected poems concerns only his youth.

III

The Ship in the Desert and *The Baroness of New York* having received scant notice in the press, Miller in the late 1870's and early 1880's undertook a new genre—drama. To his delight, his first play became one of the most popular plays of frontier life. Adapted from *First Fam'lies* and entitled *The Danites in the Sierras,* it was revised by a Philadelphia actor, Alexander Fitzgerald, for production by the McKee Rankins. Its first night was on August 22, 1877, at the Broadway Theatre in New York. After numerous long runs in various cities, the Rankins took the play to London in 1880, where it enjoyed nearly equal popularity. From it Miller earned a small fortune and a new esteem in New York society.

Extending over a period of time far exceeding that of *First Fam'lies,* the story of the play is characterized by incredibly rapid action. In Act I, the Widow appears in the mining camp as a missionary and immediately befriends Billy Piper, an effeminate lad protected by Sandy. In Act II, the Danites, or Mormons, "hungry, Bible-howlin' varmits," appear as Hickman and Carter; they are executioners who seek an opportunity to kill the Widow because of her father's part in the death of the prophet Joseph Smith. The Judge and Limber Tim wed the compassionate and ne'er-do-well prostitutes, Captain Tommy and Bunkerhill. Sandy proposes to the Widow, who accepts. The Widow discovers that Billy is a transvested Nancy Williams, an emigrant girl who, having escaped the Mountain Meadow Massacre, seeks to elude the Danite pursuers. Billy leaves by a window as Carter and Hickman enter by the door, only to be sent away by the Parson, who suspects they are sluice robbers. In Act III, the mining camp has become a small town with a new preacher and many gossiping women who note the friendship of Mrs. Sandy and Billy. Suspecting Billy of being a Danite, the vigilantes chase him into Mrs. Sandy's cabin. She hides him. When Hickman enters, he knifes both Mrs. Sandy and her newborn babe, then exits. Since Billy has no knife, he is exonerated. In Act IV, Hickman threatens Billy with a half-exposed knife and departs. When it appears that Billy might die because of his illness, Sandy promises to bury him "by the side" of the Widow. Hickman then returns with the vigilantes; the Parson recognizes his voice, pulls off his false beard, and declares the Danite to be the Widow's murderer. Billy then identifies himself and weds Sandy, who, normally inarticulate, makes an actual speech to conclude the play:

> SANDY (*to Nancy*) . . . We don't mean bad; but it's a rough country, and we're rough, and we've not been good to you. But there is an old and beautiful story in the Bible—(*to audience*)— you've all heard it before you learned to read, I reckon. It is of that other Eden. There the living God met man face to face, communed with him every day in his own form. And yet that man fell. Well, now, we don't claim to be better than they were in Eden, even in the heart of the Sierras.[28]

To its viewers, the play offered not only rapid action and suspense, but also sentiment and humor. The Parson reflects on the Widow's presence: "When I see'd that 'ere little widder a bendin' over a wash-tub, earnin' her bread by the sweat of her brow . . . well, I thought of my mother and my sister, an' it made me better—better—and I loved her so, I loved her so."[29] Captain Tommy weeps as she addresses the Widow: "Widder, between us rolls a wide river that has borne Bunker and me from the high, sunny shore where you stand to the dark, muddy t'other side; and I'll not try to cross it, widder."[30] The Judge's dialect speech and his irrepressible malapropisms provide much of the humor. He objects to the coming of a missionary—"It's in-sinervatious, that's what it is."[31] He provides news of the Parson's travels: "Why, he went away north to Frazer River; got smashed up in a mine there I hear; washed through a flume and his limbs all broke up till he had as many joints as a sea crab."[32] He tells of Tim's success: "Mr. Limber Tim's member of the Legislature now, wife, family name Bunkerhill, of the Bunkerhills of Boston." [33]

Miller's second play, *Forty-Nine—An Idyl Drama of the Sierras*, produced by the Rankins in New York in 1881, was his second and last play to reach a wide audience. It has the same appeal as *The Danites* in action, suspense, and humor. Its melodramatic, ludicrous sentiment would be difficult to surpass. When Snowe, an old lawyer friend of the Devine family remarks, "Charley! Charley! You are drinking again. You will break your old mother's heart," Charley replies, "My mother! Don't say a word to *her!* I—I—will reform to-morrow."[34] Though his mother cries, "No! No! Not there!," Charley leaves for the Sierras, from which his father has not returned though he had left many years be-fore. It is there in a gambling house that he meets Carrots, an orphan girl who sings to provide bread for her protector, poor old Forty-nine.

Carrots has much of the attractiveness of Mollie Wopsus. Innocent, inquisitive, forthright, she is, according to Forty-nine, "24 carats fine, and all pure gold" though she's "got no dignity, but lots of heart." She does not have Charley's idolatrous rev-erence for mothers: "O please, I don't like mothers. If old Mississip is a specimen, I tell you they are tough citizens."[35] Forty-nine himself cannot bear to talk about Charley's mother when Carrots prods him:

CARROTS. Weren't you never young? And didn't you love no girl, like me?
'49. Yes, yes, yes.
CARROTS. And she didn't love you back?
'49. She did! God bless her!
CARROTS. And why didn't you marry her, then?
'49. I did—I did! Now, Carrots, you're liftin' up the water gates, and you'll flood the whole mine.

Later she quizzes Charley in much the same way about Belle, the beauty of the gambling house:

> CARROTS. And you used to like her, didn't you? You used to try to get close to her, and say things, didn't you? You liked her, and she liked the other feller. That's just always the way. Nobody never likes anybody that anybody likes.
> DEVINE. O, set the table. I never loved Belle.
> CARROTS. You never loved her?
> DEVINE. I did, and I did not. [Charley proceeds to speak of man's love "as the vine climbing feebly up to the sun . . . lays hold with its tendril on whatever it can; be it foul or fair, the heart of man takes hold of the highest nature that comes near him. . . ."]
> CARROTS. Hey?
> DEVINE. You don't understand?
> CARROTS. No; that's all Modoc to me.[36]

Carrots fortunately retains her delightful character to the end:

> '49 (to Carrots). You are to be my child.
> DEVINE. And my wife.
> CARROTS. Oh! Charley!
> SNOWE. You are a great heiress.
> CARROTS. Then I am somebody in particular![37]

This play is significant in that Carrots, as a forerunner of Mollie Wopsus, becomes through Henry James's *Daisy Miller* a prototype of the "real American girl." Indeed, Miller's drama has little other interest nowadays. It is little more than a curious exhibit of popular nineteenth-century American comedy, a rollicking and tearful entertainment without substance and without serious purpose.

visited the author in the late 1880's, rode off with one of his horses, was arrested for housebreaking in Portland, Oregon, and sentenced to the Oregon State Penitentiary at Salem for a two-year term. After serving five months, Henry escaped from the Prison Farm and returned to California. On December 9, 1891, the California newspapers carried the story of the boy's holding up a stagecoach near Ukiah and of his later capture. The clue to his identity was a letter found near a woodpile where he had worked addressed to "Joseph McKay" and signed "Your brother, George B. Miller." The letter was dated from "The Hermitage, Oakland Heights," the poet's home later renamed simply "The Hights" (he insisted on this spelling). Upon conviction of robbing the United States mails, "Harry" Miller was sentenced to two years at San Quentin. At the expiration of the term in 1893, he was returned to the Oregon State Penitentiary from which he was finally released in 1895. During these years Miller was the object of widespread public criticism: he was the "Poet-Lothario" who had deserted his sweetheart and abandoned a "poor, deserted motherless boy."[2]

In 1897 he made bigger headlines. News from Yukon and Alaska gold fields filled column after column in North American newspapers: reports of miners arriving in Seattle with thousands of dollars in gold dust; descriptions of major routes to the Klondike; speculation about possible famine in Dawson City; news of sailings, hardships, trading companies, labor shortages, mail problems, and mining methods. The United States Secretary of Agriculture promised an experimental farm by the Yukon. Frank Corey of Kalamazoo, Michigan, announced a balloon trip to Alaskan gold fields. The director of the Geological Survey declared that a railroad from Montana through the Yukon to the Bering Sea would be feasible. Mrs. Laura Morton of Paris, Illinois, told of plans to leave her two young sons that she might serve homemade bread and pies to homesick Klondike miners.

From July to November, 1897, Joaquin Miller was probably the nation's most noted argonaut. Letters of his voyage from Seattle to Dawson City were purchased for exclusive publication in newspapers owned by W. R. Hearst, but actually other newspapers printed them. Hearst threatened to sue Joseph Pulitzer's

New York *World* because of its appropriating the prized correspondence. A total of eighteen letters was published. Now almost forgotten, they represent some of Miller's best journalistic writing.

At the outset Miller anticipated a glorious adventure. He would tell "the cold, frozen truth" about the Klondike, the mines, and the miners. He would stake a claim himself and wield pick and shovel. He would prove that the poor man, with forty pounds of equipment and supplies, could make the trip from San Francisco to Dawson City for as little as one hundred dollars. He would respond poetically to the "vast solitude and primeval wilderness." Above all, in the "virgin freshness" of America's greatest unexplored territory, he would renew his youth. He would scale the Chilkoot, descend the Yukon, and participate in the greatest rush of half a century. Though sixty years of age, he protested that he was no visionary, that he knew his strength.

Without waiting for a special Hearst expedition to be organized, Miller boarded a Southern Pacific train for Seattle, booked passage on the steamer *City of Mexico,* and wrote his first letter on July 26 "on the water and away from the rush, rattle, and roar of insane Seattle." However, the steamer was so packed with four hundred gold-seekers that he found his elbow "jostled all the time." But it was a happy ship of decent, companionable folk.

From the start Miller was skeptical about the validity of reports predicting starvation in the gold fields. He estimated that so many ships plying the Yukon could each deliver so many thousand pounds of supplies to Dawson City. He noted that *Klondike,* in Indian dialect, means "plenty of fish." He believed wild game would be plentiful: "One man returning from the mines told me this morning that he always had to keep the bacon up on a high pole and had to grease the pole, for the bears were so bad that they would tear the cabin down, and even climb the pole if they could. Now it seems to me," said Miller, "that while the bear up the pole was eating the bacon a man of reasonable wisdom could get a little of the bear if starving."[3]

On July 30, Miller for the first time viewed Alaska. He found the grandeur of the Inside Passage difficult to describe adequately: "Ten o'clock and the sun is still shining in the snow dappled hills and peaks of Alaska. The high black hills right and left are as spotted as Jacob's cattle. Steep canons of snow shelter down almost to the water's edge here in the last days of July. We are passing away from under the path of the sun. It is already cool, cold, a savor of frost is in the air from the fields of snow about us, above us. We are steaming up a mighty gorge, a vast, still river, wide and dolorous and deep."[4] He was delighted by the industry of the Indians on Annette Island; he was glad to hear that they were getting rich by operating a sawmill and that they needed no help from the white man. He expressed a sentimental kinship for the people of Juneau; they had endured hard times in the search for gold. Skagway, he found, was congested with miners at the mercy of an entrepreneur with whiskey and town lots for sale.

Chilkoot Pass left Miller utterly exhausted. He had scarcely sufficient strength to write of the scenery he had seen, of a "hundred Yosemites" with "glaciers looming over and hanging down out of the clouds on either side of the trail."[5] By the shore of Lake Linderman on the Canadian side of the summit he was met by Hearst correspondent Edward Livernash, who reported that "our dear old Joaquin . . . was all but dead and so weak that he could not lift one leg over the other. When he wished to shift his position at the fire we had to render him assistance."[6]

He traveled twelve days by barge down the Yukon with mountains all about: "Mountains on top of mountains, mountains in line with mountains, a monotony of sky-companioned mountains. But it is the monotony of the stars; a monotony of majesty and magnificence."[7] His party caught fish, but larger game—even bears—was not to be found. From Dawson City he traversed the Klondike from Bonanza Gulch to Sulphur Creek to view the mines and to converse with miners. His last letter, written on September 13, reported that Dawson City was snowed under.

He intended to proceed down the Yukon and to return to San Francisco on October 20. However, he got no farther than Circle City, Alaska. He staked a claim, found no riches, and left abruptly after several days to verify a report that men were starving on the trail between Circle City and Dawson City. Accompanied by a friend, he pulled his supplies on a sled over the trail, mile after mile, hoping to prepare a story for Hearst. He nearly lost his own life as a result of snowblindness and frostbite; he and his companion were rescued by an experienced musher who took them to a Dawson City hospital where Miller convalesced for several weeks. These events the *Washington Standard* noted briefly on the first page of its January 14, 1898, issue: "The 'Poet of the Sierras' has met with misfortune in the Eldorado. On a trip from Circle City to Dawson, he lost part of the great toe of his left foot and his left ear from being frozen. Both cheeks were likewise nipped by the borean blasts."

Six months later and with little fanfare Miller slipped back to "The Hights." Fortunately, in headline news the Spanish-American war had superseded the Klondike. Miller had earned $6,000 from Hearst for his letters, but he had not brought back thousands of dollars in gold dust. Moreover, he had been a poor prophet in predicting adequate food and supplies during the 1897-98 Yukon winter. There is no cheer in his poem "Alaska," in its reflection of icy, gloomy immensity:

> Ice built, ice bound and ice bounded,
> Such cold seas of silence! such room!
> Such snow light, such sea light confounded
> With thunders that smite like a doom!
> Such grandeur! such glory! such gloom!
> Hear that boom! hear that deep distant boom
> Of an avalanche hurled
> Down this unfinished world!
>
> Ice seas! and ice summits! ice spaces
> In splendor of white, as God's throne!
> Ice world to the pole! and icy places
> Untracked, and unnamed, and unknown!
> Hear that boom! Hear the grinding, the groan
> Of the ice-gods in pain! Hear the moan
> Of yon ice mountain hurled
> Down this unfinished world.[8]

Alaska, his last great adventure, was to be a renewing of his youth and a recollecting of his youthful days in California and Idaho mines. The Chilkoot and the Yukon both overwhelmed him; his stamina was unequal to the test he gave himself. His mountain was topped, but with greatest difficulty; he "faced the four winds with the face/Of youth," but his retaining youthful vigor was a fantasy he promoted to the end of his days.

He was at peace with the world. In *Life Amongst the Modocs*, he had said: "These Indians burn their dead. I have looked into this, and, for my part, I should at the last like to be disposed of as a savage."[9] On his estate he built his own funeral pyre. When he died, he was cremated and his ashes placed on the pyre. He had also directed that preachers of every denomination officiate at his memorial services; but, as the San Francisco *Call* put it, "This was found inexpedient." The Unitarian minister who gave the funeral address spoke of "the last of America's great poets." The *Call* declared that "Columbus" was comparable to Lincoln's Gettysburg address and greater than Emerson's "Concord Hymn."

In life, Miller was aware of such esteem; but perhaps he would have appreciated most the words of his mother. Before her death in 1905 she assured one visitor solemnly and confidentially that her son was "greater than Shakespeare."[10]

II

Many stories are told about Miller's handwriting. He normally used a quill pen. He said it "fitted his mood" because it made "a big, broad track."[11] In making his own quills, he unfortunately used a dull knife. Consequently, his penmanship, poor at best, was nearly undecipherable when he wrote with a quill. Ina Coolbrith claimed she had copied whole books of Miller manuscript for his printers.[12] Harr Wagner, another California friend, claimed that both he and Thomas Nunan prepared Miller's Alaska and Yukon correspondence for the composing room of the San Francisco *Examiner* and other Hearst newspapers.[13] Many of Miller's acquaintances, including Walt Whitman, left Miller's letters unanswered simply because they could not read them. Perhaps the best story, reported in the Indianapolis *News* of October 28, 1913, concerned an invitation Miller received to attend a meeting of a literary society. Because his reply was illegible, the secretary of the society wrote a second time to request that he make a cross at the bottom of the letter if he were coming or a circle if he were not. Miller, it is said, complied with the request; but nobody could decide whether the mark he made was intended for a circle or a cross.

Throughout his adult life Miller indeed made "a big, broad track." There was no unanimity about him—whether he was a great genius, whether he was a good and noble man, whether he could write genuine poetry, whether indeed his writing (legible or not) was ever really comprehensible. Miller was his own best publicist: he played the role of the Western hero in his early poetry and prose and in London society, and he often reprinted favorable excerpts of British reviews of his work. For the most part, the British viewed him kindly and curiously more for what he seemed to represent than for the art of his prose and poetry. Literary critics in America who knew the West were especially hostile. Upon the publication of *Songs of the Sierras*, Bayard Taylor wrote General Edward F. Beale as follows:

> My dear Beale: Thank you heartily for writing, as well as sending me your defense of Kit Carson, and scarification of that vulgar fraud, Joaquin Miller! I am very glad to have my own immediate impression confirmed. The fellow really knows nothing about the life he undertakes to describe, and this is the "great American poet" of the English literary journals. Why, I'd undertake to write a volume of better and truer "Songs of the Sierras" in three weeks. We authors have really fallen on evil days when such stuff passes for poetry. However, patience is my watchword; we have but to wait and see these fictitious reputations go down as fast as they go up.[14]

Samuel A. Clarke commented in a "Letter from Oregon," in the September 27, 1872, issue of the Sacramento *Union:*

I read the first part of the "Isles of the Amazon" with uncertainty, not failing to realize that there were numerous gems of thought and fancy to be found there, and striving to be oblivious to all his sins of omission and commission, the chief of which, perhaps, was that he hackneys his own conceits by such constant repetition of them that they become a surfeit to our taste and amount to weakness of illustration. Poetical license may palliate what is unreal, and even improper, once, but it nauseates when you discover that what you supposed was a trivial fault has been adopted by the poet as "style," and is evidently claimed as "originality." I cannot refrain from an expression of regret that this last production is so crude in expression, careless in versification, and at times so hackneyed in tone, illogical, unreal, and even false as well as sensuous occasionally as to deprive it of claims to great and lasting literary fame.

On May 3, 1873, the *San Francisco Newsletter and California Advertiser* observed that "Joaquin Miller has a fine natural sense of the sound of words, with but a feeble sense of their value. . . . His greatest effort, 'Arizonian,' is perfectly unmeaning."[15] In his home state of Oregon, memories of his "desertion" of Theresa Dyer were kept alive; when his fourteen-year-old daughter Maud was arrested in Portland in April, 1879, for attempted "abduction," that city's *Oregonian* used the occasion to publish an editorial entitled "In Fine Frenzy Rolling," a broadside attack on Miller's poetry.[16] The two plays, *Danites in the Sierras* and *Forty-nine*, the book *Songs of the Soul*, his Alaskan adventure, lecturing, and the collected *Poems* all contributed to his becoming an author to be read in schools and to his becoming a subject of hagiography and reminiscence for at least ten years after his death.

Today Bayard Taylor's prediction has come to pass. Rarely is Joaquin Miller read. Rarely is he the subject of scholarly study. But the silence is not altogether deserved. In the future, Miller will not recover a great reputation for belles lettres. He will be rediscovered only in small ways. His accounts of skirmishes with the Indians in Northern California and Oregon may be quarried from old newspaper files to give a renewed sense of immediacy to an era that is now long past. His influence in seeking justice for the American Indian in "a century of dishonor" may yet be determined. His debt and contribution to great writers of his time will make an illuminating study. But, above all, Miller will be most rewardingly viewed as a man who promoted a legend about himself, a legend reflecting an American dream of epic adventure in days of frontier life.

Notes and References

Notes and References

Chapter One

1. Manuscript diaries, The Honnold Library. The comment was written on December 27, 1857, while Miller was at Columbia College.

2. Oregon Historical Society Library newspaper scrapbook. Date and name of newspaper not identified.

3. Manuscript diaries, The Honnold Library.

4. *Ibid.*

5. *Joaquin Miller: His California Diary*, edited by John S. Richards (Seattle, 1936), p. 57.

6. Manuscript diaries, The Honnold Library.

7. See his account in *The Battle of Castle Crags* (San Francisco: The Traveler, n.d.), and Gibson's statement in *Joaquin Miller's Poems* (San Francisco, 1909), IV, 98.

8. See *Joaquin Miller: His California Diary*, pp. 17-53 passim.

9. See *Memorie and Rime* (New York, 1884), pp. 81-87 passim.

10. "Colonel Baker as a Poet," San Francisco *Call*, August 28, 1892, p. 9. Baker and Delazon Smith visited Columbia College while Miller was a student there. See also Perry D. Morrison, "Columbia College, 1856-60," *Oregon Historical Quarterly*, LVI (December, 1955), 327-51.

11. Manuscript diaries, The Honnold Library.

12. *Shasta Courier*, June 18, 1859, p. 2. A file of this old newspaper is found in the Redding, California, public library.

13. *Ibid.*, July 23, 1859, p. 3.

14. Named Cali-Shasta; after her mother's death, she was reared by Ina Coolbrith in San Francisco.

15. See "The Poet of the Sierra," San Jose *Pioneer*, April 27, 1878, p. 1. The article is reprinted from the *Golden Era*.

16. Court of Sessions, Siskiyou County, II, 85.

17. First published in the *Democratic Register*, March 15, 1862; republished as late as August 30, 1862.

18. Manuscript diary, Yale University Library.

19. See letter of General Wright in *Oregon Statesman*, October 13, 1862, p. 2.

20. Letter to the Editor, *Golden Era*, July 19, 1863, p. 4. Joaquin's letter is occasioned by the publication of his poem, "Cape Blanco."

21. Marriage certificate, Oregon Historical Society Library.
22. Reported in San Francisco *Call*, September 26, 1872, p. 1.
23. *Ibid.*
24. Manuscript letter, University of Oregon Library.
25. See Miller, "Joseph E. Lawrence," San Francisco *Call*, September 4, 1892, p. 13.
26. See Miller's account in San Francisco *Chronicle*, April 8, 1883, p. 1.
27. See "How I Came to Be a Writer of Books," *Lippincott's*, XXXVIII (1886), 106-10.
28. Reported in San Francisco *Call*, September 26, 1872, p. 1.
29. These comments are in the ledgers now in the Oregon Historical Society Library.
30. Archives, Oregon State Library.
31. These incidents are reported in Fred Lockley's column, "In Early Days," *Oregon Journal*, March 3, 1915.
32. A partial file of *The Daily Mountaineer* is available in the Oregon Historical Society Library.
33. *Memorie and Rime*, p. 217.
34. Manuscript letter in Oregon Historical Society Library.
35. Reported in San Francisco *Call*, October 26, 1872, p. 4.
36. *Memorie and Rime*, pp. 217-18.
37. Archives, Oregon State Library.

Chapter Two

1. Quoted in Portland *Oregonian*, February 19, 1913.
2. Quoted in *ibid.*, August 28, 1915.
3. This copy is owned by Miss Joaquina Miller, Miller's daughter by his wife, Abigail Leland.
4. Quoted in Portland *Oregonian*, February 19, 1913.
5. Charles Warren Stoddard, *Exits and Entrances* (Boston, 1903), pp. 224-25.

Chapter Three

1. *Overland Monthly*, IV (January, 1870), 104.
2. Manuscript essay, The Bancroft Library.
3. *Ibid.*
4. *Ibid.*
5. *Songs of the Sierras* (London, 1871), p. 299.

6. "California's Fair Poet," San Francisco *Call*, August 21, 1892, p. 14.

7. Miller's spelling.

8. *Songs of the Sierras*, p. 6.

9. *Songs of the Mexican Seas* (Boston, 1887), p. 133.

10. *Songs of the Sierras*, p. 10.

11. *Ibid.*, p. 169.

12. *Songs of the Sun-lands* (Boston, 1873), p. 21.

13. *Ibid.*, p. 102.

14. *The Ship in the Desert* (Boston, 1875), p. 205.

15. *Ibid.*, p. 28.

16. *Ibid.*, p. 160.

17. *Ibid.*, p. 191.

18. Introduction to *Joaquin Miller's Poems*, I, 119.

19. *Life Amongst the Modocs* (London, 1873), p. 21.

20. See "A card from Joaquin Miller," *San Francisco Newsletter and California Advertiser*, October 7, 1871, p. 3. Miller states: "I formed my estimate of the man when I had but little to love. . . . 'A tall man,' I believe, in the old term, as used by poets, did not always imply a man of uncommon stature."

21. *Life*, p. 296.

22. *Ibid.*, p. 319.

23. *Ibid.*, p. 438.

24. *Ibid.*, pp. 334-35.

25. Quoted in Henry Nash Smith, *The Virgin Land* (New York, 1957), pp. 119-20.

26. Quoted in *Joaquin Miller's Poems*, I, 120.

27. *Ibid.*

Chapter Four

1. *The One Fair Woman* (New York, 1876), p. 196.

2. *Ibid.*, pp. 222, 266, 315.

3. *Ibid.*, p. 353.

4. *Ibid.*, p. 12.

5. *Ibid.*, p. 90.

6. *Ibid.*, p. 547.

7. *Ibid.*, p. 380.

8. *Ibid.*, pp. 206, 217.

9. *Ibid.*, p. 354.

10. *Ibid.*, p. 159.

11. See Leon Edel, *Henry James: The Conquest of London* (Philadelphia, 1962), p. 298. Edel concludes that Alice Bartlett told James the story of Julia Newberry, the "child of nature and freedom."

12. *The Ship in the Desert*, pp. 25-26.

13. *The Baroness of New York* (New York, 1877), pp. 25-26, 42.

14. *Songs of Italy* (Boston, 1878), p. 162.

15. *Life Amongst the Modocs*, pp. 210-12.

16. *Songs of the Sierras*, pp. 44, 50.

17. *Joaquin Miller's Poems* (San Francisco, 1909-10), III, 21-22.

18. July 8, 1871, p. 832.

19. Oscar Wilde, *Decorative Art in America* (New York, 1906), p. 25.

20. George Wharton Hubbard, *So Here Then Is a Little Journey to the Home of Joaquin Miller* (East Aurora, New York, 1903), pp. 29-30.

21. *The Poetical Works of Joaquin Miller*, ed. Stuart P. Sherman (New York, 1923), p. 539.

22. *Ibid.*, p. 534.

23. *Ibid.*, p. 540.

24. *Ibid.*, p. 532.

25. *Joaquin Miller's Poems*, I, 155.

Chapter Five

1. *Joaquin Miller's Poems*, I, 151-52.

2. *Ibid.*, I, 154-55.

3. *Ibid.*, I, 153-54.

4. *Songs of the Sierras*, pp. 28, 29. The second couplet was deleted in Miller's revision of 1909.

5. *Joaquin Miller's Poems*, V, 190.

6. *Songs of the Sierras*, p. 180.

7. More detailed comparisons are made in Gabriella Brendemuhl, "Joaquin Miller's Indebtedness to Byron" (unpublished M.A. dissertation, University of Chicago, 1921), pp. 19-23.

8. *Songs of Italy*, p. 83.

9. *Ibid.*, p. 11.

10. Martin S. Peterson, *Joaquin Miller, Literary Frontiersman* (Stanford, 1937), pp. 143-45, cites "sounds sweet as the voice of a singer/Made sacred with sorrows unsaid" from "Isles of the Amazons" and "Where winter winds from warm Cathay/Sing sibilant" from "The Larger College."

11. *The Poetical Works of Joaquin Miller*, p. 438.
12. *Ibid.*, pp. 419-20.
13. *Joaquin Miller's Poems*, III, 13.
14. *Ibid.*, I, 156.
15. "How I Came to Be a Writer of Books," in *My First Publication*, ed. James D. Hart (Book Club of California, 1961), p. 39.
16. *Memorie and Rime*, pp. 40, 43, 47.
17. *Ibid.*, p. 10.
18. See "To Russia" and "To Rachel in Russia," in *Joaquin Miller's Poems*, I, 158-59, 162.
19. See "Cuba Libre" in *ibid.*, I, 163-64.
20. *Chants for the Boer* (San Francisco, 1900).
21. *First Fam'lies in the Sierras* (London, 1875), pp. 54-55.
22. *Ibid.*, pp. 63-64.
23. *Ibid.*, p. 69.
24. *Shadows of Shasta* (Chicago, 1881), p. 127.
25. *The Destruction of Gotham* (New York, 1886), p. 7.
26. *Ibid.*, p. 31.
27. See M. M. Marberry, *Splendid Poseur: Joaquin Miller—American Poet* (New York, 1953), pp. 167-68.
28. *Joaquin Miller's Poems*, VI, 61-62.
29. *Ibid.*, VI, 20.
30. *Ibid.*, VI, 23.
31. *Ibid.*, VI, 10.
32. *Ibid.*, VI, 48.
33. *Ibid.*, VI, 49.
34. *Ibid.*, VI, 68.
35. *Ibid.*, VI, 96.
36. *Ibid.*, VI, 97, 101-2.
37. *Ibid.*, VI, 120.

Chapter Six

1. *Joaquin Miller's Poems*, V, 193.
2. See Oregon State Penitentiary Records, Nos. 2338 and 3041, Oregon State Archives; San Quentin Prison Register, MS Vol. 1244, No. 14783, State of California Archives; San Francisco *Call*, December 9, 1891, 1:8; San Francisco *Examiner*, September 10, 1893, 3:5. The boy baptized Henry Mark is recorded as John Miller in inmate records of the Oregon State Penitentiary; Harry Miller in San Quentin records; Harry Miller alias Joseph McKay in the *Call;* and Hall Miller, alias James Miller, in the *Examiner*. A letter to the Governor

of California from Mrs. S. V. M. Brown, dated April 26, 1895, asked a pardon for the young man based on Joaquin Miller's desertion of his family. Apparently, from the Oregon State Penitentiary, where Henry Mark was released February 22, 1895, he was returned to Alameda County, California, authorities to be further sentenced.

3. "Sing of the Klondike," Chicago *Tribune*, July 29, 1897, p. 4.

4. "As Joaquin Miller Sees It," Chicago *Tribune*, August 7, 1897, p. 1. Reprinted in "To Chilkoot Pass, 1897," ed. O. W. Frost, *Alaska Review*, II (Spring and Summer 1966), 43. The *City of Mexico* struck a rock and sank north of Queen Charlotte's Island on the return voyage, August 5, 1897.

5. "Roses on the Trail," Chicago *Tribune*, August 27, 1897, p. 3.

6. "Are Over the Pass," Chicago *Tribune*, August 20, 1897, p. 5. According to Livernash, Miller told him: "Son, there is a weariness that reaches in and squeezes the spirit till it shrinks. I have it, but, peril, I love thee, and dare thee, and I cannot be suppressed."

7. "Down on the Yukon," Chicago *Tribune*, August 29, 1897, p. 3.

8. *Joaquin Miller's Poems*, IV, 109.

9. *Life Amongst the Modocs*, p. 276.

10. Hubbard, *op. cit.*, p. 16.

11. Quoted in Portland *Oregonian*, August 24, 1913.

12. Undated manuscript letter, Ina Coolbrith to Blanche Partington, Bancroft Library.

13. *Joaquin Miller and His Other Self* (San Francisco, 1929), p. 176. Miller and Wagner were co-editors of the *Golden Era* in 1886. Wagner served as Miller's agent in negotiations with W. R. Hearst. Wagner's book reprints Miller's diary, October 26 to December 5, 1897, covering the period of the perilous trek from Circle City to Dawson City. See pp. 179-90.

14. The letter is dated August 27, 1871, and is reprinted in Fred Lockley's column, "In Early Days," *Oregon Journal*, March 3, 1915. Beale was surveyor general for Nevada and California.

15. "Mr. Joking Miller," p. 8.

16. May 21, 1879. Judge M. P. Deady of Portland had mailed Miller a news item from the *Oregonian* reporting the arrest of Maud. Miller immediately left the East, arriving in Portland on May 19. In an interview he told an *Oregonian* reporter, "You have ruined the character of that child. You have used this childish freak to ruin me" (*Oregonian*, May 20, 1879, p. 3). The offending story appeared in the *Oregonian* of April 30, in which it was reported that Maud Miller

confessed to cutting the hair of a twelve-year-old girl friend and to conspiring with T. E. L. Logan to dress her in boy's clothing and to send the girl by steamer to San Francisco. Maud was in Portland for a six-weeks' theatrical production. T. E. L. Logan was her foster father, having married Theresa Dyer Miller in 1877. He received a jail sentence; Maud was placed in the custody of her father, who now succeeded in becoming her legal guardian. Miller placed her in a convent school in Canada. At this time Theresa Dyer Logan was separated from her husband and living in San Francisco.

Selected Bibliography

Selected Bibliography

PRIMARY SOURCES

1. Books

Specimens. Portland, Oregon: Carter Hines, 1868.

Joaquin et al. Portland, Oregon: S. J. McCormick, 1869.

Pacific Poems. London: Whittingham and Wilkins, 1871.

Songs of the Sierras. London: Longman, Green, Reader, and Dyer, 1871; Boston: Roberts Bros., 1871.

Songs of the Sun-lands. Boston: Roberts Bros., 1873.

Life Amongst the Modocs: Unwritten History. London: Richard Bentley & Son, 1873. Revised and published under various titles, including *Unwritten History; Paquita;* and *Joaquin Miller's Romantic Life Amongst the Red Indians.*

First Fam'lies in the Sierras. London: G. Routledge, 1875. Revised in dramatic form as *The Danites in the Sierras.*

The Ship in the Desert. Boston: Roberts Bros., 1875

The One Fair Woman. London: Chapman and Hall, 1876.

The Baroness of New York. New York: G. W. Carleton, 1877.

Songs of Italy. Boston: Roberts Bros., 1878.

Songs of Far-away Lands. London: Longman, Green, Reader, and Dyer, 1878.

The Danites in the Sierras. Chicago: Jansen, McClurg, 1881.

Shadows of Shasta. Chicago: Jansen, McClurg, 1881.

Forty-nine. San Francisco: The California Publishing Company, 1882.

Memorie and Rime. New York: Funk and Wagnalls, 1884.

'49: The Gold-Seekers of the Sierras. New York: Funk and Wagnalls, 1884.

The Destruction of Gotham. New York: Funk and Wagnalls, 1886.

Songs of the Mexican Seas. Boston: Roberts Bros., 1887.

In Classic Shades and Other Poems. Chicago: Belford-Clarke, 1890.

The Building of the City Beautiful. Chicago: Stone & Kimball, 1893.

An Illustrated History of the State of Montana. Chicago: Lewis Publishing Company, 1894.

Songs of the Soul. San Francisco: The Whittaker & Ray Co., 1896.

As It Was in the Beginning: A Poem. San Francisco: A. M. Robertson, 1903.

Light: A Narrative Poem. Boston: H. B. Turner, 1907.

Joaquin Miller's Poems. 6 vols. San Francisco: The Whittaker & Ray Co., 1909-1910. Autobiographical essay in Volume I.

The Poetical Works of Joaquin Miller. Edited by Stuart P. Sherman. New York: G. P. Putnam, 1923. Excellent introductory essay.

Overland in a Covered Wagon: An Autobiography. Edited by Sidney G. Firman. New York and London: D. Appleton, 1930.

Joaquin Miller: His California Diary. Edited by John S. Richards. Seattle: F. McCaffrey at his Dogwood Press, 1936.

2. *Other Published Sources*

The writings listed below are not included in Miller's books.

Alaska and Klondike Correspondence. Chicago *Tribune,* July 26, 28, 30, 31; August 2, 3, 10, 16, 25, 29; September 4, 13, 1897; January 23, 30; February 6; May 1; July 10, 20, 1898. The same correspondence appeared in the San Francisco *Examiner,* the New York *Journal,* and in numerous other newspapers.

"A Brief Campaign." San Francisco *Chronicle,* April 8, 1883, 1:1-2. Miller's leadership in an Indian war in Oregon in March, 1864.

The Battle of Castle Crags. San Francisco: The Traveler, 1894. 20 pp.

"California's Fair Poet." San Francisco *Call,* August 21, 1892, 14:6-7. Ina Coolbrith.

"Canyon City Pickles—No. 5," The Dalles *Daily Mountaineer,* August 25, 1865. This issue is in the Oregon Historical Society Library.

"A Card from Joaquin Miller." *San Francisco Newsletter and California Advertiser,* October 7, 1871, p. 3. Miller claims he saw General William Walker.

Chants for the Boer. San Francisco: The Whittaker & Ray Co., 1900. 28 pp.

"Charles Stoddard." San Francisco *Call,* August 14, 1892, 12:3-4.

"Colonel Baker as a Poet," San Francisco *Call,* August 28, 1892, 9:3-4.

"Dante Gabriel Rossetti." San Francisco *Call,* December 18, 1892, 11:1-2.

Democratic Register, Vol. I, Nos. 2, 10, 16-20, 22, 24, 25, 28. March 22 to September 20, 1862. Oregon Historical Society Library. No. 29, the last number, September 27, 1862, is in The Honnold Library.

Eugene City Review, Vol. I, Nos. 1, 2, 5-16. November 1, 1862, to February 14, 1863. Oregon Historical Society Library.

"George Eliot." San Francisco *Call,* December 11, 1892, 13:1-2.

Selected Bibliography

"Helen Hunt Jackson." San Francisco *Call*, September 18, 1892, 11:7-8.

"How I Came to Be a Writer of Books." *Lippincott's*, XXXVIII (1886), 106-10.

"J. Ross Browne." San Francisco *Call*, October 30, 1892, 11:4-5.

"Joaquin Miller: Sedition and Civil War." Edited by John R. Dunbar. *Pacific Historical Review*, XIX (February, 1950), 31-36. Editorial reprinted from *Democratic Register*, September 27, 1862, in The Honnold Library.

"Joseph Lawrence." San Francisco *Call*, September 4, 1892, 13:7-8.

"Klondike Gold, 1897." Edited by O. W. Frost. *Alaska Review*, II (Spring and Summer, 1967), 20-39.

"Letters of Joaquin Miller." Edited by Beatrice B. Beebe. *Frontier*, XII (1932), 121-24, 223-28, 344-47. Letters to George M. Miller.

"London on the Surface." San Francisco *Call*, February 5, 1893, 13: 6-7. Miller's first day in London, 1870.

"Lord Byron." San Francisco *Call*, December 4, 1892, 13:5-6.

"Lord Houghton." San Francisco *Call*, January 8, 1893, 14:1-2.

"Mrs. Frank Leslie." *Golden Era*, XXXVI (May, 1887), 180-83. Lily Langtry became Mrs. Leslie.

"On and About the Avon." *Overland Monthly*, VII (October, 1871), 325-31.

"Pit River Massacre." San Francisco *Chronicle*, March 25, 1883, 1: 1-2; and April 1, 1:1-2.

"Prentice Mulford." San Francisco *Call*, August 7, 1892, 9:3-4.

"A Ride Through Oregon." *Overland Monthly*, VIII (April, 1872), 303-10.

"Robert Browning." San Francisco *Call*, November 27, 1892, 14:5-6.

"Rome." San Francisco *Call*, February 26, 1893, 14:4.

"Rough Times in Idaho," *Overland Monthly*, V (September, 1870), 280-86.

A Royal Highway of the World. Edited by Alfred Powers. Portland, Ore.: Metropolitan Press, 1932. Miller's diary of the trip to Canyon City, 1864.

"Scenes in Central England." *Overland Monthly*, VI (May, 1871), 409-18.

"Some Letters of Joaquin Miller to Lord Houghton." Edited by Clarence Gohdes. *Modern Language Quarterly*, III (1942), 297-306.

"Swinburne." San Francisco *Call*, December 25, 1892, 13:7-8.

"To Chilkoot Pass, 1897." Edited by O. W. Frost. *Alaska Review*, II (Spring and Summer, 1966), 43-54.

"To London." San Francisco *Call*, November 27, 1892, 14:5-6.

Trelawney with Shelley and Byron. Pompton Lakes, N.J.: Biblio Co., 1922. 24 pp. Reprinted from San Francisco *Call*, January 29, 1893, 14:1-2.

3. *Manuscripts*

Diaries, 1854-1858. The Honnold Library. These include letters, poems, and schoolwork.

Diary of Henry Cummins. Yale University. Cummins was a printer for Miller's *Democratic Register* in July and August, 1862.

Grant County (Oregon) Script Receipts, Book A, 1865-1869. Oregon State Archives.

Indictment for Assault, January 7, 1860, Court of Sessions, Siskiyou County (California), Vol. II, p. 85.

Ledgers 4, 5, 6, and 7, 1864-1869. Oregon Historical Society Library. These include financial records, manuscript copy for *Specimens* and *Joaquin et al.*, speeches, and reflections.

Letters to Blanche Partington. Bancroft Library. Twenty-five letters, 1897-1910.

Letters to Ina Coolbrith. Bancroft Library. Twelve letters, 1906-1912.

Letters to M. P. Deady. Oregon Historical Society Library. Four letters.

Marriage Certificate, C. H. Miller and Theresa Dyer, Curry County, September 12, 1862. Oregon Historical Society Library.

Suit for Divorce, Theresa Miller and C. H. Miller, April 4 and 18, 1870, Circuit Courts of Coos and Lane Counties. Oregon State Archives.

Tribute to Joaquin Miller by Ina Coolbrith. Bancroft Library.

SECONDARY SOURCES

BRENDEMUHL, GABRIELLA C. "Joaquin Miller's Indebtedness to Byron in Connection with His Early Narrative Poems." Unpublished dissertation, University of Chicago, 1921. An excellent study.

"California's New Poet," *San Francisco Newsletter and California Advertiser*, August 5, 1871, p. 2. The anonymous writer was one of Miller's classmates at Columbia College and editor of a rival newspaper in Eugene.

DYKES, MATTIE M. "Joaquin Miller: A Biographical Study." Unpublished dissertation, University of Chicago, 1922. Miss Dykes corresponded with George M. Miller and with William Thompson, Miller's classmate at Columbia College and a boarder in the Miller home, 1862-1863.

HAIGHT, MARY M. "Joaquin Miller in Oregon, 1852-54 and 1857-70." Unpublished dissertation, University of Washington, 1936. Miss Haight uses Miller's diaries, 1854-58 and extensive secondary sources.

HUBBARD, ELBERT. *So Here Then Is a Little Journey to the Home of Joaquin Miller,* East Aurora, New York: The Roycrofters, 1903. Reminiscence of Miller at "The Hights."

KEISER, ALBERT. "Joaquin Miller," *The Indian in American Literature.* New York: Oxford University Press, 1933. Miller's defense of the Indian.

LORCH, FRED W. "A Note on Joaquin Miller," *American Literature,* III (1931), 75-78. Miller at Columbia College.

MARBERRY, M. MARION. *Splendid Poseur: Joaquin Miller—American Poet.* New York: Thomas Y. Crowell, 1953. A biography viewing Miller unsympathetically; especially detailed concerning his visits to London, his friendship with Lily Langtry, and his last years in California.

MORRISON, PERRY D. "Columbia College, 1856-60," *Oregon Historical Quarterly,* LVI (December 1955), 327-51.

PETERSON, MARTIN S. *Joaquin Miller, Literary Frontiersman.* Stanford University Press, 1937. Only book-length criticism of Miller's work of any real worth; generally too high an estimate of the intrinsic value of his work.

"The Poet of the Sierra," San Jose *Pioneer,* April 27, 1878, p. 1. Story of Miller's outlawry in California, 1859-1860. California Historical Society Library.

POWERS, ALFRED. "Joaquin Miller," *History of Oregon Literature.* Portland, Ore.: Metropolitan Press, 1935. See also "Minnie Myrtle Miller." Oregon newspaper sources for poetry and biography; compares wife's poetry favorably with Miller's.

READ, FRANK R. "Cincinnatus Hiner Miller: A Critical Biography." Unpublished dissertation, University of Virginia, 1926.

STODDARD, CHARLES WARREN. "The Poet of the Sierras," *Exits and Entrances.* Boston: Lothrop, 1903. Stoddard's friendship with Miller from 1869.

THOMPSON, H. C. "Reminiscences of Joaquin Miller and Canyon City," *Oregon Historical Quarterly*, XLV (1944), 326-36. Stories favoring Theresa Miller from persons who knew the Millers.

VEATCH, GLEN E. "The Indiana Boyhood of the Poet of the Sierras," *Indiana Magazine of History*, XXX (June 1934), 153-60. Land transactions of Hulings Miller in Grant County, Indiana, are discussed.

WAGNER, HARR. *Joaquin Miller and His Other Self*. San Francisco: Harr Wagner, 1929. An anecdotal biography by a friend who with Miller was co-editor of the *Golden Era* in 1886.

WALTERHOUSE, ROGER R. "Bret Harte, Joaquin Miller, and the Western Local Color Story." Unpublished dissertation, University of Chicago, 1939.

WEIRICK, BRUCE. "Joaquin Miller and the West," *From Whitman to Sandburg in American Poetry*. New York: Macmillan, 1924. A brief guide to the poetry; themes in Whitman and Miller compared.

WILDE, OSCAR. "Joaquin Miller, the Good Samaritan," *Decorative Art in America*. New York: Brentano's, 1906. Wilde quotes from his correspondence with Miller.

Index